BTCV

ENVIRONMENTS FOR ALL

THE BTCV GUIDE FOR COMMUNITY ACTION

Chris Church

with Emily Cluer and Rhiannon Guy

A Think Book for BTCV

Text © Think Publishing 2005
Design and layout © Think Publishing 2005
The moral rights of the author have been asserted

By Chris Church
with Emily Cluer and Rhiannon Guy

BTCV
Conservation Centre, Balby Road, Doncaster DN4 0RH
Registered Charity 261009

Think Publishing
The Pall Mall Deposit
124-128 Barlby Road, London W10 6BL
www.thinkpublishing.co.uk

All rights reserved. No part of this publication may be reproduced, stored in a retrieval system,
or transmitted in any form or by any means, electronic, mechanical, photocopying, recording
or otherwise, without the prior permission of the copyright holder.
A CIP catalogue record for this book is available from the British Library.

ISBN 0 946752 36 2

Printed by Cambridge Printing
This book is printed on paper of which at least 30% comes from well-managed forests
independently certified according to the rules of the Forest Stewardship Council, 30% is from
post-consumer recycled waste paper and 10% from mill waste.

The publishers and authors have made every effort to ensure the accuracy and currency of the
information in Environments for All..

DISCLAIMER: The information given in this publication on behalf of BTCV is believed to be correct,
but accuracy is not guaranteed and the information does not obviate the need to make further
enquiries as appropriate. This publication is not a comprehensive statement on all safety
procedures and the reader must take all reasonable steps to ensure the health and safety of all
users and to take all necessary steps to implement a health and safety policy. This publication is
issued without responsibility on the part of BTCV for accidents or damage as a result of its use.

Acknowledgements

The materials in this handbook are based on the experiences of the many organisations that took part in the 'Environments For All' programme. The text also refers to and is informed by a range of materials produced for people to use by BTCV, some of which can be found on the BTCV website, www.btcv.org. Thank you to all those who have contributed case studies and special thanks to Ben Proctor for advice and assistance.

acti/e
communities

ENGLISH
NATURE

BTCV is very grateful to The Home Office Active Communities Directorate and to English Nature for their support in the production of this book.

About BTCV

BTCV is the UK's leading practical conservation charity. BTCV connects people with place, builds healthy, sustainable communities, and increases people's life skills. It aims to create a better environment where people from all cultures feel valued, included and involved. BTCV supports 140,000 volunteers a year taking hands-on action to improve their urban and rural environments, and a Community Network supports local groups. BTCV offers regular conservation tasks, UK and International Conservation Holidays, the BTCV Green Gym®, training opportunities and an on-line shop making products and services accessible to all..

BTCV is one of the largest deliverers of the Millennium Volunteer's programme (MV) working with 16–24 year olds to encourage young people, some of whom are school excluded, to get involved in volunteering action of their choice. MV Placements allow volunteers the chance to experience different working environments, gain training and develop new skills.

Individual members and affiliated groups of BTCV receive the *Conserver* magazine, and have access to advice on many aspects of conservation volunteering, including organising a local group, health and safety advice, grants and insurance. For further details please contact the Community Groups Unit at:
BTCV, Conservation Centre, Balby Road, Doncaster DN4 0RH
Tel: 01302 572244 E-mail: information@btcv.org.uk

For local volunteering opportunities, please call:
01302 572244 (England)
02890 645169 (Northern Ireland)
01786 479697 (Scotland)
02920 520990 (Wales)

Call customer services on 01302 572244 for information on getting involved in:
BTCV Conservation Holidays, BTCV People's Places Award Scheme, BTCV Training, BTCV Green Gym, BTCV's Millennium Volunteers, BTCV's Community Group Network, Tools plants and handbooks

INSPIRING PEOPLE, IMPROVING PLACES

Contents

Foreword

 Sustainable development is, for me, the only intellectually robust framework within which we can combine people's legitimate aspirations for economic progress and a safe society, with the opportunity to develop their own internal well-being, and protect the world around them. BTCV's contribution to this is enormously important, helping to provide people with a sense of place, security, well-being, participation and purpose.

This book will help you play your part in this empowerment. Using as its platform BTCV's successes with their Environments for All programme in particular, it will help you to discover new ways and new ideas for energising, facilitating, running and participating in community projects that will truly make a difference to the immediate environments in which you and the people around you live.

What do I mean by 'environments'? Most people think that the environment is everything that happens outside our lives. We're *here*, and the natural world is over *there*. Yet this is a huge philosophical error creating a false divide between us and the physical world. We need to change our mindset here, to view our world as being us *in* the environment, not us *and* the environment. And the only way we can do this is to acknowledge that the environment is rooted in our own sense of place: our homes, our streets, our neighbourhoods, our communities.

The work of BTCV is encouraging a new approach, an approach that this book will help encourage. Not nimbyism, but 'imbyism'– yes, do come into my back yard, let's get things done, let's not mess around any longer. This work is a hugely important antidote to the chronic disempowerment that blights people's inner lives today, and simultaneously makes their lives the poorer in terms of the quality of their physical environment.

As this book shows, BTCV is not just at the heart of Environments for All, but is beginning to add new dimensions to what it means in practice. The more BTCV continues developing its ideas and helping people open up their worlds, the better it is for all of us. With this book, you too will be able to explore new and exciting ways of improving environments for all.

Jonathon Porritt

Jonathon Porritt
Chairman, UK Sustainable Development Commission

How to use this book

This book will give you everything you need to know about getting involved in local community action, from starting a community group to making sure that everyone can be included. It anticipates the problems from setting up a project through to monitoring and publicising it.

To help you along the way you will find case studies from the last three years of Environments for All (EfA). These are examples of EfA projects and appear in case study boxes.

If you would like any further information on any of these EfA projects or would like to discuss your ideas on practical environmental action with disadvantaged communities, please contact BTCV on 01302 572244.

Please note that BTCV Green Gym®, mentioned throughout this book, is a registered trademark.

Part 1
Introduction

'We're all environmentalists nowadays.'

Politicians have said this many times in the last 20 years. But is it true? Most people do say they care, but if you look at the state of our towns and our countryside you may end up thinking that perhaps they don't care very much.

Perhaps it's not so much a matter of caring about the environment as doing something about it. An opinion poll in 2002 showed that 77% of people in the UK were worried about the state of the environment, but a survey for the Co-op Bank showed that only about three per cent were actually doing anything to help.

Why don't people take more action to protect and improve our environment? There may be all sorts of reasons (lack of time and so on), but a few issues stand out:
- People don't know what to do;
- People don't know how to get involved; and
- People lack the confidence to get involved.

But there's another important reason to add to these: all too often many people feel left out and excluded. Environmental action often seems to be about complicated scientific issues, or appears to be only carried out by well-off, well-educated people.

In reality that's not the case, but that perception is one reason for the Environments for All programme. Environments for All (EfA) was set up in 1999 by BTCV to develop its work to encourage and support people from all backgrounds and communities, regardless of race, gender and social circumstances, to get involved in action to improve their environment.

BTCV has worked to explode the myth that people from ethnic minorities and other marginalised groups are not interested in taking practical environmental action, and has provided people with opportunities to take that action in ways that suit them best.

BTCV recognised that it is not enough just to say that their programmes and projects are 'open to everyone' – many people need support and guidance if they are to get actively involved. BTCV was already a large organisation, with over 130,000 people taking part in voluntary activity every year, and an estimated 250,000 people in associated community groups. But for many people the organisation had an image of mostly male and mostly white people, doing conservation work out in the countryside.

This has never really been the case: more than half BTCV's work takes place in urban areas and local communities, but it was true that the majority of it was done by white, relatively affluent, able-bodied volunteers and that it was rare to see people from minority ethnic groups active on environmental issues.

Over the last five years, EfA has promoted new ways of working. It has focused on reaching people who have traditionally felt marginalised or excluded from this kind of work, and has also worked to encourage those in existing projects to think more about how they work with the people who live in and around the places where they work. The work has been independently assessed and evaluated, and it has certainly done a lot to start to change the face of environmental participation.

This guide is based on what has been learnt in these five years. It's here to provide advice and inspiration to anyone who wants to work at a local level to create better places to live. You'll find the advice in Part Two: it covers key issues about setting up local projects, getting everyone involved and making sure the projects work well. Hopefully the case studies will provide the inspiration: there are over 40 examples throughout the guide to represent just what can be done. There are also plenty of references to guidebooks, websites and other sources of information. This isn't a book to be read through from start to finish and then forgotten: we hope that it will be a useful reference guide, especially to the specific points covered in each chapter of Part Two.

What do we mean by 'the environment'?

For many people the environment has been something we watch on television; we are fascinated by gorillas and killer whales, or perhaps are worried by reports of global climate change. But it can all seem a long way away: it's pretty rare that our notion of 'the environment' seems to have much to do with where we live.

There's another contradiction that can make things confusing: much of what we hear about in the news covers national and global environmental policy, and that seems to have very little to do with making things better on our own streets. Similarly, those people who are trying to improve things locally, whether though conservation, waste recycling or better cycle facilities, may not have much influence on the people who make the local and national policies.

But it isn't just the 'green' environment that is important. We may worry about environmental issues such as transport or air pollution in our area, but young people die every year in every neighbourhood from road accidents: if it's happening down our streets doesn't that make it an environmental issue? Too often environmental priorities seem to be defined by an expert or a politician rather than by people who are living in poor conditions. When this happens it's not surprising that people feel that the environment has 'nothing to do with me'.

Sometimes concern about such local issues is criticised. Local protesters complaining about new developments are seen as 'NIMBY's (Not In My Back Yard). But if I don't care about my back yard, then who will? Perhaps the challenge for us all is to recognise that there is a link between what happens where we live and what happens on a global scale.

We also need to recognise that everyone has a different 'sense of place'. We all have places that we care about – places where we live, places that we think of as our home, favourite places to visit or simply landscapes that we've only visited once, but are ones we immediately feel are special. These are important parts of 'our environment' and they are different for everyone.

So EfA has three challenges:
● To make environmental action accessible to everyone;
● To widen our perceptions of what we mean by the environment; and
● To link local action with the global picture.

What is 'sustainable development'?

The press and politicians started talking about 'sustainable development' after the 1992 United Nations 'Earth Summit'. It was the main focus of the follow-up event 10 years later in Johannesburg. The United Nations defines sustainable development as 'development which meets the needs of present generations, without compromising the ability of future generations to meet their own needs'. At the core of this idea is the necessity for meeting people's needs – for housing, for clean water, for a employment, for education for their children, for good health care, and for a safe and healthy neighbourhood in which to live.

People have many different needs, but at a local level they can usually be grouped together into three broad areas:
● Better social conditions;
● A better local economy; and
● A better local environment.

It's worth thinking about what sustainable development means literally. Development means change or growth; sustainable means things that last. This is about making changes that last, about making things better now and in the future.

It's also about tackling these issues together. For instance, new shops are unlikely to open (which would help improve the economy) in an area where crime and poverty levels are very high (poor social conditions). Similarly crime is unlikely to fall in an area where local green spaces and housing have been improved unless there are also jobs to be had. People may move into an area where housing and jobs are available, but if the local environment is unpleasant and polluted they may well not want to stay.

Sustainable development is about working now for a better future. This is also the priority for action at a local level: there's little point in putting time and effort into improving your local recreation area if six months later it is desolate and vandalised.

Can local action really make a difference?

This is a valid question: sometimes our local efforts can seem unimportant in comparison to national and global problems. This is why it's also easy to think that these problems are something that should be dealt with by politicians. But, if politicians don't see any evidence that people care about the issue, they're hardly likely to treat it as a priority, and sitting round waiting for someone else to solve your problem is never a good use of anyone's time!

Local action does make a difference, and connecting local actions makes an even bigger difference. For example, in 2002, community furniture recycling projects (which repair and refurbish old furniture and electrical equipment and sell it on to people on low incomes) found new homes for over a million items that would otherwise have been dumped in landfill sites around the UK.

What has EfA achieved so far?

Between 2000 and 2004 over 38,000 people in 1,176 community groups benefited directly from the support that's available to them through the EfA programme, and about 183,000 benefited indirectly. The focus throughout has been on the people who are often left out, from the poor and elderly to refugees, ex-offenders and people with disabilities and long-term illnesses.

An analysis of 152 projects showed that EfA involved a very wide range of people in 2002:

People with health problems	19%
Other socially excluded people	16%
People with disabilities	15%
Black and minority ethnic people	13%
Older people	13%
People living in poverty	9%
Offenders and ex-offenders	8%
Young people at risk	4%
Asylum seekers and refugees	3%

However, it's not just about working with individual people. There's plenty of community spirit in the UK too. The Community Development Foundation estimates that there are around 700,000 community groups across the UK, of all shapes and sizes, from well-funded associations with several staff to tiny mother and toddler groups, from anglers and book clubs to youth clubs and even amateur zoologists... People come together because they have shared interests, and all of them help to create a better community.

BTCV works with many of these groups. In Northern Ireland, the EfA programme has set up groups from different faiths and many local communities, such as the Belfast Travellers' Support Group and the Chinese Welfare Association. Nationally, BTCV has built partnerships with organisations such as Age Concern, The Muslim Council, the Sensory Trust and the Refugee Council. The Black Environment Network has also played an important role in this work by reviewing the programme annually.

Many of the EfA projects have been on a small scale. No one project can transform any community and changes do not take place overnight. It may well take several years to make real lasting changes to an area and the way people do things in it. But if we're trying to create more sustainable communities, then that long-term view is vital, and the only way to get that to work is to make sure that the people living in the area where the work is being done know what's going on, help plan it and become part of it.

Moving on – creating stronger communities

There's always going to be a need for local people and groups to look after the places where they live. The last 10 years have seen the number of people involved in local action on the environment treble across the UK. That's wonderful, but there's always more to do. Research shows that many of the people who would like to be involved may be uncertain about how they can help and where they should start.

Sometimes the hardest thing to do is taking that first step: talking to other people, going to a meeting, deciding that 'something must be done!'.

Once you do it, you may be surprised at how many other people will feel the same way and want to help.

The lesson from these case studies (and from many others) is that local action works: there are thousands of examples all over the UK. It's not just about high-profile campaigns: it's often simply local people getting organised to turn run-down and polluted areas into attractive places for relaxation and recreation. This kind of local action is not just about the environment. It also helps people get to know their neighbours, it helps people discover and use skills they didn't know they had, and it can certainly help build stronger and more sustainable communities.

Our countryside and our urban open spaces are under pressure from inappropriate economic development and perhaps always will be. Pollution regulations and planning controls can only do so much: when it comes to the crunch, it is only action by local people that will be able to protect the places and the environment we need and enjoy.

Part 2.1
Getting started

This section looks at:
- Why organise a local project?
- How do we know it will work?
- How do we get started?

Why organise a local project?

The essence of EfA is pretty simple. It is that everyone can get involved in practical action to improve his or her environment and local quality of life.

But getting involved isn't as simple as it sounds. People can only get involved when:
- There is some form of local action or a project to get involved in;
- They are aware that this work is going on;
- They can see that the work is interesting and is going to help make things better; and
- They can see that there is something that they can personally achieve.

Therefore, setting up a new project isn't just about identifying something that needs doing. It's about careful planning, and it's about working out how to work with and involve people. This is a skill that can be learned just in the same way as driving a car or using a computer.

Specialist professionals may need to be brought in for certain project tasks. They should be fully integrated into the group, as a well-planned local project or programme can help to build the skills of local people, so that by the end they're doing things they had never thought they could do at the start.

CASE STUDY: GETTING STARTED IN OLDHAM

It's not too difficult to get a brand new project going. Cath Crowley is a Community Project Officer in Oldham who had to start from scratch: 'I started by ploughing through lots of volunteer lists. There was a lot of running around, meeting people and finding out what aspects of the environment would appeal to them.' Cath saw from her research that food was socially and culturally very important, and decided to use this as a starting point: 'We started running training sessions for Asian ladies interested in growing food on the allotments. We are now trying to develop this interest further into other environmental issues.'

Since then the project has:
- Set up a Green Gym in urban Oldham working with rangers from the countryside service which involves members of different ethnic communities.
- Organised orienteering and problem-solving activities for boys and girls from Oldham Bangladeshi Youth Association at local country parks.
- Run nature rambles, environmental crafts, pond dipping, mini-beast hunting, miniature pond creation and visits to an RSPB reserve and an aquarium for local children.
- Organised a trip to the Centre for Alternative Technology (CAT) in Wales for a group of local children, followed by a renewable energy workshop during their school half-term holidays.
- Helped upgrade and improve the Shaheed Minar memorial garden with Oldham Bangladeshi Youth Association.

The commonest reason for organising a local project is because something is crying out to be done! It may be that green spaces on an estate have become a focus for fly-tipping, that an underpass linking two neighbourhoods is unsafe and unfriendly, or that newly-arrived young refugees need opportunities for community integration. Indeed, it can be just about anything that inspires people to take action!

If you're part of a community group you may want to tackle an issue yourselves; on the other hand you may decide you need support from a local conservation or environmental group, or from your local council.

If you're a professional working with such a group it may be that a new project comes up from the grass roots in this way. It may also be that a new project comes to you from another agency such as a local council or as a development of work that you or colleagues have recently completed.

It doesn't always matter too much exactly where the idea for a project comes from. The aim is after all to improve the places people care about. But it is important if you are working with local people that you make sure that what is planned has local support, if not from everyone, then certainly from the people it will affect.

How do I know my project will work?

The answer is simple: you don't! There are thousands of small projects aimed at improving local life set up every year, and sadly a fair number of them fail to deliver or simply fail to get going.

However, good planning can cut your chances of failure to a minimum. To help your project succeed, you should:

Make goals realistic and achievable

If you're working with a small group new to practical action don't try and transform your whole neighbourhood. Focus on something that people are happy and confident with, and about which they think 'yes, we can do that!'. A quick win will boost people's confidence and motivate them to go on to bigger things.

Involve local people effectively

Getting local people involved in planning and delivering a project takes time and effort and money. (see Part 2.2). But spending that time is important: it will help ensure that the project meets people's needs; it will get more people involved; and there's also plenty of evidence to show that 'community-owned' projects suffer less vandalism.

Prepare a good action plan

This may sound very obvious, but plenty of groups don't begin their projects with proper plans. You need to start with a process in place, with a clear idea about how you will begin, what happens next, the order of work, and so on. Contact your local BTCV office if you think you need further advice. If you are working on a specific piece of land you will also need to develop a site plan showing exactly what you will do.

CASE STUDY: THE CALTHORPE PROJECT ON GRAY'S INN ROAD, LONDON

The Calthorpe Project is a community garden that has existed since 1984 when local residents campaigned against the sale of the land for development, and transformed it into a valuable community garden and educational resource. Dumping and burning had left contaminated soil and disfigured trees, but volunteers, including local youths, replanted the garden.

Now it is an important community project in the heart of London's Kings Cross urban sprawl, providing a real green haven in an otherwise concrete neighbourhood. As well as enhancing urban biodiversity, this community garden is also a neighbourhood asset, as it gives diverse groups of people the space to meet and socialise, making the green spaces both productive and aesthetically pleasing. It is both an urban oasis and an educational resource for the local community on recycling and ecological awareness.

In 2002, BTCV's People's Places programme funded the building of a greenhouse here. It was designed by a local architect, Robert Bishop, to fit in with the local surroundings and to withstand vandalism. It was built entirely with the help of volunteers, and is central to several projects in the garden, each of which work with a diverse selection of community groups, including adults with learning difficulties, volunteers, local residents and children. Groups who benefit include the Bengali Women's Garden Group, the Kids Environmental Club and local families from many ethnic minorities in the area who use the greenhouse to grow herbs and vegetables. It also provides a centre for accredited horticulture training.

However, the Project was about much more than just a new greenhouse. It involved some of the same local youths who had vandalised the original

greenhouse. As Robert Bishop explained: 'The greenhouse project demonstrated that "self-building" is an effective way of conferring ownership, and therefore a degree of responsibility upon a place. The "owners" of the greenhouse were drawn from those youths who had contributed to the destruction of the previous greenhouse, as well as groups with a background of long-term unemployment and groups with learning difficulties.'

The process created a new sense of life within the Project. Its construction, and more importantly, its method of construction, has addressed the tension between local youth and Calthorpe. This tension has now dissipated and progressed to a positive new atmosphere. The sense of ownership from the youth volunteers has diminished the level of vandalism.

A second People's Places award from BTCV is now going to help volunteers get involved in the planning process and construction of other new buildings, including a workshop, which will make use of recycled materials for experimenting on and developing construction methods. The workshop will build a number of structures, and volunteers will be trained to use the equipment – skills which they can then use to find employment. Plans also include a sensory garden for small children and the construction of a community classroom from recycled materials.

Monitor and evaluate as you go

Too often people don't evaluate what they do enough, and if they do, it's usually not until the end. Building good monitoring and evaluation processes into your project from the start (see Part 2.8) will give you the ability to deal with little problems before they become big ones.

Make your budget cost-effective

You need to have a clear idea of where your money is going. It's not a matter of how much money you have – small projects can be just as (or more) effective as larger ones – but whatever money you have needs to deliver real change (see Part 2.7 for more ideas).

How do I get started?

One of the key issues for anyone responsible for a neighbourhood or a local area is simple: how well do you really know the area?

If you're a long standing local resident, it may be easy to say 'very well', but even people who've lived in one place all their lives may miss important issues because they've got used to things being the way they are. If you're new to the area, you need to research the place thoroughly. If you don't do this you're likely to be seriously embarrassed when people start talking about places or issues you know nothing about.

Therefore:
- Start with local people – ask them to give you a guided tour on foot, and don't be scared to ask lots of questions;
- Check the background data: one easy way to do this is by feeding postcodes into www.upmystreet.com where you'll find a lot of useful information;
- Talk with local community workers, whether they're in the nearest community centre, with the council, or in an agency like SureStart (which works on education and children) and Connexions (young people). Phone them or visit their offices. If they're busy, make an appointment to visit later. And don't forget the police, local schools and local religious groups – they can all provide good local knowledge;
- Find out if there are other similar projects active in the area (or ones that have closed or finished recently) – who is/was involved in these? What do/did they do?;
- Walk around by yourself (or with a friend if you don't feel safe);
- Look at the state of the streets and the open spaces;
- Look at the advertisements for events that are in shop windows;
- Ask yourself what it would be like to live here – would you like it?;
- Examine what the facilities are like – the shops, the schools, the religious buildings, the pubs, the post office and so on;
- Make a note of the names of the main roads;
- Check out the public transport links; and
- Find out if there's a library in the area, and spend some time there checking the local materials collection.

Even two hours spent like this will give you a much better feel for an area.

In 2001, a newly formed Tenants & Residents Association on the Hilltop estate in Ebbw Vale decided to tackle the problems affecting their community and run-down green spaces around them. They approached BTCV Cymru for help and the local BTCV Community Project Officer offered the support and guidance needed to help the group get started to make their estate and surroundings greener, cleaner and safer.

The first step was a 'Snapshot' photographic project. This helped people record the areas around the estate that were crying out for change and also documented what local people wanted to change in their neighbourhood. Out of this exercise, the group developed an action plan which gave a framework to decide how best to improve the area. This also enhanced community pride and created a sense of ownership.

The group were keen to take on a large 10-hectare site but began by gaining valuable experience on a smaller scale project, creating a new garden for the estate. The first step was to receive permission to use the site from the local council and the BTCV Community Project Officer offered advice and support to help the group deal with the technical and legal issues. This equipped the group with the skills to begin work. Once work began, support and guidance was given on fundraising, sourcing match funding and effectively involving and motivating the community to take an interest in their estate. A group evaluation was undertaken which helped everyone involved understand more about their achievements, as well as providing the knowledge needed to expand and get more people involved in the project.

Despite the illness of some group members, the project has become self-sustaining. The project has also provided a framework for local people to work within, giving them confidence to continue to maintain their newly created green spaces by themselves. As the BTCV Community Project Officer explained: 'The group has overcome some dreadful traumas associated with health problems. The fact that they are still going and working on the project is a tribute to their group spirit and tenacity. This is true community spirit and it is alive and well in Hilltop.'

Environmental assessment

Looking around the local area will give you a good picture of the place and the people, but its environmental issues may not be so obvious. What looks like overgrown wasteland to some people may be a refuge for small animals or an important habitat for butterflies for others. Similarly, derelict industrial land may have some nasty secrets if it has been used for waste dumping in the past or was the site of polluting activity, such as a gas works. This is very important to know if you're intending to create a site where children will play or vegetables might be grown. The planning department of your local council will also be able to give advice on previous land uses.

If you're planning a major project, these things matter, and the best thing to do is to get some outside advice if you're at all unsure. A first stop for such advice may well be your local BTCV office: if they can't help they'll probably know someone who can. There is also likely to be a Local Biodiversity Action group or Partnership, made up of organisations, specialists and interested local people who will know which habitats are important in your local area.

This kind of assessment may take time and cause delay, but it does matter. Firstly, because there's not a lot of point in making the environment look nicer if you've actually made it worse for the resident wildlife. Secondly, because many grant-making bodies will need to know the answers to these questions about environmental issues before they allocate any grant to your work.

With the help of some good advice you should be able to find ways to produce a 'win-win' solution – one that meets local needs and improves the overall environment.

Starting work – choosing a project

There are a lot of different ways to find a place to start practical action:

Often it will find you! Many local projects start because there's a real and obvious need to do something about a particular problem site, and local people get fired up about it. Maybe it's an obvious site such as a run-down recreation ground, but it may also be a bit of land ignored by the local council and other agencies, but known all too well to local people as an unsafe and unpleasant blot on the local landscape. Either way, the local feeling is that 'something should be done' and people look around for support and help (and find you!).

It may be one person's bright idea People can live alongside a patch of land for years and tolerate or ignore it. But then one day someone takes another look or hears that there's a new way to get money for local improvements and has the 'bright idea'. It's important if someone approaches you for help on a project like this to make sure it really is a good idea and not just one person's hobby-horse that no-one else in the area likes. This will need some community consultation (see Part 2.2).

It may come from local consultation If you're working with local people and there's a recognition that the surroundings are not all they could be, then a discussion or planning meeting may come up with some clear ideas for improvements. This needs planning and organisation (see Part 2.2), but such a meeting may produce several ideas for action. It's then up to the people involved to work out what the priority is.

Ideas may come from 'on high'

Several good local projects have come about when local groups have been approached by the local council or other landowners, who want to see some improvements in the area, and are prepared to fund work to see things happen. It may be up to you to act as an 'intermediary' – someone linking the community and the professionals – to ensure that this top-down approach is going to be popular with local people or to get it improved so that it does.

Whatever you're planning, you need to make sure that what is planned is okay with local people. You also need to make sure it's good for other species. A tumbledown garage block may look like a derelict pile of concrete and corrugated iron to most people, but to the person who's carried out the wildlife survey, it may be home to rare insects, bats or other animals. See the part above on Environmental Assessment for more ideas on this.

Who owns the land?

Perhaps you've identified a piece of land that you would like to see improved: it may be that you simply want it cleaned up, want a new playground, or you think it would be a great conservation area.

Conservation Volunteers Northern Ireland (CVNI) have developed a range of techniques to engage with the Chinese community in Northern Ireland. This Chinese community is dispersed predominantly through Belfast and Bangor, and with 8,000 members, represents the largest minority ethnic group in Northern Ireland.

Working in association with the Chinese Welfare Association (CWA), CVNI first examined the barriers to their participation in environmental activities. These included language, the geographical spread of the community and the lack of ownership of any green spaces where work could be carried out.

Building on this they then organised a series of workshops and talks on practical environmental issues which were translated into Cantonese and Mandarin. Transport is also provided to a training centre where classes are run in traditional willow sculpture. Environmental workshops also involve children by making bird feeders, planting trees and wildflowers and a host of environmental games.

The sessions provide an excellent opportunity to meet new people, share new experiences and simply have fun. They have proved to be a successful catalyst in strengthening links with the Chinese community and stimulating interest in future practical environmental activities. Environmental workshops are also organised regularly at the CWA's after school club in Belfast.

But whatever your use, someone owns that land and you will need to seek their permission.

It may be obvious who owns it or it may not. If a company hundreds of miles away has somehow come into owning a small piece of land for which they have no plans (and this happens) then it's not surprising it's an overgrown dumping ground. All land belongs to someone (in theory!) and if the local council cannot help, then the Land Registry can usually tell you who owns the bit you're interested in.

LAND REGISTRY

Before you can start a project on a piece of land you need to find out who the landowner is in order to get permission to work on their land. To do this you can contact the Land Registry Office. It's a little bureaucratic, but given that they keep records of who owns almost all the land in England and Wales, perhaps that's not surprising.

For England and Wales:
To find the identity of a landowner from the Land Registry Office you will firstly need to fill out an SIM (Search of Index Map) form. There are two ways to get this form:

1. Download it from www.landregistry.gov.uk. It can be found under the 'Publications/Forms' menu and then 'Forms' menu.

2. Phone the Land Registry enquiry line on 020 7917 8888 You can request for an SIM form to be sent to you, free of charge.

Once you have a SIM form you need to fill it out and submit it to the relevant regional office, along with a plan of the area you want to work on outlined in red.

To find out which office is the local Land Registry office, you can look at Practice Guide 51. To get hold of this you can either download it from the website, www.landregistry.gov.uk (select the 'Publications/Forms' menu, then the 'Leaflets' menu and then the 'Practice Guides' menu), or you can phone the enquiry line (020 7917 8888) and ask for one to be sent to you.

When the SIM form has been filled out and sent in to the Land Registry Office, the application will be processed and the title numbers for the land in question will be sent to you. This is free of charge, unless the number of titles returned on your search is over 10. In this case there is a charge of £4 per title. So 9 titles are free; 10 titles are free; 11 titles cost £4; 12 titles cost £8; and so on. If your search returns more than 10 titles, you will be informed by the Land Registry office and asked to pay the fee. They can then send you the title numbers.

Tip: Applications can often be broken down into several smaller ones covering a smaller area that will be more likely to return less than 10 titles.

Once you have the title numbers you can use this information to find the identity of the landowner. You will need to fill out an OC1 form. This can be found, on the website (www.landregistry.gov.uk)

under the 'Publications/Forms' menu and then 'Forms' menu on the website. Alternatively, you can phone the Land Registry enquiry phone number (020 7917 8888) and they will send you a copy.

Once you have filled out the OC1 form, send it to the relevant local Land Registry office and if there is a registered landowner they will send you a copy of the register (£4) and the title plan (£4). It is then your responsibility to contact the landowner to get permission to work on their land.

The Land Registry office only covers registered land. It is possible that the landowner will not be registered. However, you should still try to discover who the landowner is. This can be done by going to the area, asking local people, asking the council and doing some footwork of your own.

For Scotland:
In Scotland, you need to contact Registers of Scotland on 0845 6070161 or check their website www.ros.gov.uk. The website has the relevant forms and plenty of guidance materials.

For Northern Ireland:
In Northern Ireland, the Land Registry operates under different legislation and its practices and prescribed forms are quite different. The starting point here is 028 90251515 or www.lrni.gov.uk.

Often it's not that difficult. The land belongs to the council, a housing association or a local business and the first step is to approach them.

Many landowners will be very happy to have a local organisation looking after their land and may even be prepared to help with small amounts of money or tools. The best way forward is to get a licence or lease, or at the very least a letter giving permission to work on the land. The Countryside Agency guide *Making Spaces* has more details on this and examples of the issues that a licence could cover.

Sometimes it is impossible to find out who owns land – usually for historical reasons. This needn't be a setback: there are perhaps 50 or more community gardens around the UK that are on land where ownership is not clear.

THE DALSTON CITY GARDEN
Keen urban gardeners in Hackney in east London spotted a piece of muddy wasteland used informally as a car park. After extensive inquiries it became clear that no-one claimed ownership. Council staff proved (informally) to be happy for them to work the land, and several of the businesses in the area supported the plan with money. Within a few months they created a small green area that did a lot to improve the surroundings.

Starting work – making plans
So far 'starting work' hasn't actually been about doing any physical groundwork. It's been about understanding the area and the issues, and about looking at places where you might work.

Even if you've got that far there's still more advance work to be done. Remember the part 'How do we know it will work?' which talks about the need for 'a good plan'. This is your next priority.

There are several questions to answer. Some of these may mean you need to look at other parts of this book, notably Part 2.5 on 'project planning'. You need to know:

- What do you want to do on the site?;
- Who's going to do the work, how many people will be involved, and what days/times suit best?;
- How much will it all cost? (if you've not got the money then you'll need this plan to help with fund-raising); and
- What are the potential problems and risks? You may well need to do a 'risk assessment' to help you decide what groundwork is feasible and to build any precautions you need to take into the costings. There is more information on this in Part 2.10.

Again, if you're new to this, you probably won't have all the answers. You may well be asking 'what is risk assessment?'. Don't let that put you off, but don't ignore the questions. There are plenty of places to go for help from local organisations, websites , council officers and local libraries. Do the planning work well, and the whole project is likely to work that much better.

CASE STUDY: JR GROUNDFORCE, BLAEN Y MAES — SWA

In 2001, the Blaen y Maes estate in Swansea had plenty of green space, but most of it was run down and poorly cared for. Green spaces are an enormous asset to any urban community, but local residents found that the run-down and neglected areas invited crime and became the focus of anti-social behaviour. Staff at the local Action Resource centre contacted BTCV with the aim of getting young people involved in environmental activities to help tackle vandalism and to install a sense of community pride and promote active citizenship by engaging the young people in community work.

The project began by working with the young people on the estate and asking them what improvements they wanted to see in their neighbourhood. They all agreed that better play facilities were required and it became clear that there was a real need for safe areas where young people could socialise. In the last three years, the initial 'informal gathering' of young people has now evolved into a powerful youth action group and youth forum with a valuable voice. Their commitment and energies have amazed all involved and their enthusiasm and dedication is contagious. The have formed the JR Groundforce, an unstoppable group which works tirelessly to blitz the estate of rubbish, and which has created no less than four community gardens. The group now has over 30 committed members between 3 and 18 years old, who meet twice a week to work on various environmental projects around the estate. BTCV's Community Project Officer for Swansea has helped them develop the skills they need including those needed for applying for funding, project management and health and safety.

The group plays a big part in the regeneration of the estate, and works in partnership with local organisations including Communities First, the local councils, a local development trust and many others. Last year they won three major community awards, including one from the Home Office and were invited to No 10 Downing Street to meet Tony Blair.

Although the area still suffers from many social problems, there is now a more supportive atmosphere. The achievements of the JR Groundforce team have proved that young people do take pride in their neighbourhoods. When given a chance to shine and an opportunity to have a say, those who once committed anti-social behaviour now proactively work against it. One of the group members, reveals all in this poem:

Us teenagers of Blaen y Maes
Us teenagers of Blaen y Maes
People say that we're not nice,
People judge us, people stare,
They all think that we don't care
Even though our lives are not fair
Most of our parents are NEVER there!!

Some turn to alcohol underage
That's why people shout and curse
Which makes us feel a whole lot worse!!

They all assume we're no good thugs
Who are nothing but trouble and just take drugs!!

We can't get jobs coz of our past
That's why we grew up too fast.

For us no-one has any time
That's why we turn to crime,
all we ask is for people to see

NOT WHAT WE ARE, BUT WHAT WE ARE
TRYING TO BE!!!!!!!!

Part 2.2
Working with local communities

This section looks at how to start to work with local people and community groups. It looks at what we really mean when we talk about 'local communities' and the key points to remember when trying to build a good working relationship. It also looks at how you can help develop effective local participation so that people can be involved in planning and managing the project, as well as carrying out the work.

If you're already active in a community then this part is for you. Some of this is aimed at people who've been active for many years, and would like to review what they're doing, or perhaps just want to find ways to work to more effectively. We can always learn more!

First steps to co-operation

If you are new to an area, remember: You need local people to trust, like and respect you. This may not be easy: they may have been there a long time and seen community workers and funding programmes come and go, leaving them with the same old problems. You need to give them good reasons to trust you, and that will involve hard work and some very careful listening. Experience is always very useful, but even if you're new to this kind of work, there are things you can do that will help make success much more likely.

There's a fair chance that your initial work in planning a project (as in Part 2.1) will have helped make links with one or more local community groups. But if you are serious about the idea of 'Environments for All', then you also need to make plans to involve as much of the local community as you can, or at least make sure that everyone has the opportunity to join your work.

Who is your 'local community'?

Even the 'local' bit is not always easy: you may be talking about a single street, a village, a neighbourhood within a bigger town, an estate or even a whole town. Other people may see things differently. A local councillor will think in terms of her or his ward – the area where the electorate lives. A regeneration agency will think in terms of the area they are funded to work in, which is often decided by some fairly complicated economic assessments such as 'indices of deprivation'. Someone who walks everywhere will have a very different idea of the 'local' to someone who drives or cycles.

'Community' is certainly difficult to define. A local authority 'Community Strategy' will cover their whole area, involving up to several hundred thousand people, but most people would see the community as 'the people who live where we live'.

It may be easiest to think of the local area as a 'neighbourhood', because communities are often a lot more than just a place.

One useful definition of community is:
A group of people with something in common – a belief, a location, a purpose, or a need – who wish to work as, or be identified as, a group for sharing, and/or mutual gain, or simply to feel that they belong.

One of the most desolate council estates in Wales, Caia Park in Wrexham made the headlines in summer 2003 when a breakdown in communication between residents and some Kurdish refugees led to rioting. A local politician compared it to the Wild West, saying: 'I think the council would have liked to fence it off and throw food in once a week.'

Its 11,000 residents are not the sort of people traditionally expected to take ownership of the environment, but BTCV has been proving that marginalised people really do care about their surroundings. For two years, BTCV Cymru has been working with the Caia Park Environmental Group and in partnership with Communities First to set up a gardening club, and it now has over 60 members.

Their goal has been to foster and focus a positive sense of pride in a community riven by mistrust and disaffection. 'I have met so many people through the club', said one woman, 'and the main thing we all have in common is that we want to make a difference to the estate, not just give up.' The workshops and other activities enable people to meet in a friendly atmosphere and have fun together as they share new experiences and learn new skills – from composting to constructing window boxes. The project has underlined the fact that there is often a direct connection between quality of environment and quality of life.

BTCV has involved residents at every stage of the planning to ensure that the club meets local needs and priorities. 'Mere consultation', said Andy, the Community Project Officer, 'is not enough. Our role is to advice and support, not dictate.'

Another crucial lesson has been the importance of clear and effective communication to resolve – or better still, prevent – conflict. 'You have to be honest and realistic about your aims and expectations', said Andy, 'and to anticipate potential difficulties at the start and plan accordingly.'

One member observed: 'There are some really decent people living here, but no one's cared about us before.' Now contact is slowly being re-established with the refugees on the estate. Plans are in hand to involve children – for example with the purchase of wormeries for local primary schools – and delegations from nearly Brynteg and Tan y Coed have visited with a view to setting gardening clubs of their own.

Perhaps the biggest achievement of the project has been to demonstrate that with proper training and support, a community can manage something like this on its own.

So think of a community as 'people with a purpose'. It's not just about where you live, but often about what you do and think.

In any locality there may be three types of community:
- Communities of place – people who live in a specific area;
- Communities of interest – people who share common interests or attributes, eg people who play football in a park, disabled people, people who live in homes managed by the same Housing Association, people from a specific ethnic group, people who work in the same place and so on; and
- Communities of identity – these defined by a shared feeling of identity or some strong common bond. Faith groups are one example.

It could, therefore, be the case that 'the community' where you may be about to start work is in fact a large number of small communities of different types and sizes, all overlapping and co-existing, with geographical boundaries that are very different for different people.

ACTION POINT
Think about and write out a list of all the 'communities' that you are a part of. Would other people see you as a part of any other communities?

We all think of the local community a little differently, particularly because communities change over time. If you are from outside an area and are just starting work there, then your view of the community will certainly be different again. For that reason it's important to start with what you know. Work with the contacts you have to try and identify the communities in the area where you want to work. It may help you to think at three levels:
a) The individual people who share the place, interest or identity;
b) The community groups in which these individuals organise; and
c) The networks which link these groups together.

All of these will be important, so it's worth spending some time trying to develop a full list. Perhaps you are only looking to work with a specific community of interest such as young people, but even then you may find different communities within that group (boys and girls for starters!).

Spotting the 'stakeholders'
If you're going to look at who is who in a community, it is also useful to think in terms of stakeholders – people and organisations who have an interest (a stake) in the area. They may not live there but they may be very important. They might include:
a) People who run a business in the area (local shop-keepers);
b) People who provide local services (council employees, the police, health service workers etc);
c) Voluntary groups based in the area, who may have staff or volunteers who live there too; and
d) Voluntary groups not based in the area but who operate there.

Some stakeholders will be very keen to work with you: they'll be in touch as soon as you are seen to start work and may attempt to convince you that their assessment of what's wrong and what is needed is the best and only solution! These may be very active local residents – be careful that you don't only listen to the people with the loudest voices. If someone who claims to represent the community contacts you, try and be sure that what they are telling you is not just their own opinion.

Other people and groups may take a lot more convincing. They may not trust you. They may have their own priorities, which you need to understand: if people are very worried about racist attacks in an area, they may not see an idea for a tree-planting project as very relevant or appropriate. Practical projects are a good way to bring a community together, but there's a lot of careful community work to be done first.

WHO ARE YOUR STAKEHOLDERS?

A list of stakeholders and community groups is a good place to start any project. Set aside some time to work with your local contacts to develop such a list: this can be a very useful exercise that will help you understand more about what is going on in an area. List as many big and small organisations and groups as possible, and then think about how you might group them. Include the name and contact details of people you know in these organisations.

CASE STUDY: PHOENIX PARK, WOLVERHAMPTON

The Prudential Grass Roots Project at Phoenix Park, Blakenhall, has revitalised a piece of wasteland, transforming it into a nature trail to provide a valuable, much-needed resource for local schools and the whole community.

BTCV, in partnership with community group Friends of Phoenix Park, has worked with local volunteers to make Phoenix Park a cleaner, greener and safer environment in which wildlife can flourish. The nature trail provides school children with access to an 'outdoor classroom', and is used for a broad range of National Curriculum studies.

Situated in a New Deal for Communities area, just over a mile away from the Prudential-owned Mander Shopping Centre, Phoenix Park has experienced high levels of crime and anti-social behaviour and a lack of community facilities, especially for sport and leisure. Local people, tired of constant drug abuse and vandalism, took action and set up a Friends of Phoenix Park community group and with funding from the Prudential Grass Roots Programme, run by BTCV, were able to tackle the problems affecting their community and environment.

Listening to people to find out what they want for their community is vital to build long-term support. Developing a community-based management plan provides a framework for local people, giving them the confidence to continue to maintain their newly created green spaces by themselves.

Phoenix Park is an excellent example of how programmes such as Grass Roots can use nature conservation to empower the community and provide a common bond between different cultures and ages.

Friends of Phoenix Park and local residents have worked with BTCV to organise a range of practical activities that have engaged the whole community. Hundreds of volunteers have taken

part and have been committed to improving the site so that everyone can enjoy it.

Activities have been designed so that every generation has the opportunity to take part, including clearing the site of fly-tipped rubbish, practical conservation tasks such as bulb and wildflower planting, ground preparation and tree planting during National Tree week, creating a nature trail for local schools and the community, and organising regular litter pick-up groups.

Blakenhall's high proportion of Asian residents have been heavily involved in the project's development, and have brought together local primary school children, youths, families and elderly residents, all of whom will benefit from this urban oasis.

Today, Phoenix Park is a safe and welcoming amenity for all the community to enjoy. The image of the park has changed forever and there has been a marked reduction in vandalism and anti-social behaviour. The community now has a real sense of ownership and confidence. The park provides a much-needed space for outdoor games and recreation in a community that shows evidence of poor health. With the introduction of the national Walk Your Way to Health scheme in 2002, the newly created pathways

attract walkers from all ages and backgrounds and can be accessed by wheel-chair users.

Phoenix Park now presents opportunities for people to learn about biodiversity, and the nature trails have become a popular and creative learning tool for school children. It is now an important green space in an urban environment.

The refurbishment of the park has also included a range of partners including Wolverhampton City Council, New Deal for Communities, Groundwork Black Country, Shell Better Britain and Ibstock Cory Environmental Trust. Work has involved improving pathways and lighting, clearing shrubs, redeveloping the car park and building a multi-purpose knockabout area, sports area, educational nature trails and an adventure playground.

The project has become the focus for achieving wider social goals amongst the community, tackling social exclusion, helping to foster local pride and ownership which leads to less vandalism, damage and littering. The improved pathway lighting has meant fewer muggings, less drug use and fewer burglaries of properties backing onto the park. The regenerated area has increased the number of people willing to use the park and this has in turn helped local businesses.

Some useful groupings might include:

a) **Organisations that you are already working with;**

b) **Organisations that you need to work with which will probably be easy to involve;**

c) **Organisations that you need to work with which may be difficult to involve;**

d) **Organisations that you would like to work with if they are interested; and**

e) **Organisations that you probably do not need to work with at present but might in the future.**

Organisations in b) and c) are the important ones, especially those in c) because those are the ones where you will need to focus your attention. Agree these lists with the people involved already and make plans as to how you will contact the ones you need.

Strategies for participation

The biggest challenge for any programme is getting people involved and active. You're far more likely to be successful if people have a chance to actually get involved in the decision-making and management of the work, rather than just being consulted or asked to turn out for an occasional afternoon's work.

If you want to get other groups and people involved in a new community project first ask yourself:

- Why do we want them?;
- How would we like them to be involved?; and
- What would they get out of being involved?

The last point is crucial – we all want to know 'what's in it for me?' If another group, with their own plans and priorities, are going to get involved in your work, then they need to be aware of the benefits to them.

This brings us to participation strategies. There are many techniques for encouraging participation from games to complex exercises. Almost all have elements in common: there is some form of 'process' (meetings, surveys, special events etc), which is usually set up by professionals (planners, project workers, local council staff) with a view to getting the opinions and perhaps the involvement of the people.

Any strategy should be clear about how the people and the professionals fit in with the process.

WHAT DO WE MEAN BY PARTICIPATION?
People often use words such as 'involvement', 'consultation', 'participation' and 'engagement' interchangeably, without clear ideas of how these processes differ. However, each has a distinct meaning, which should be taken into account when planning a project:

- **Involvement is a general word, covering all the ways in which local people take part in discussions and planning.**
- **Consultation occurs when local people are asked for their views about a proposal or a project that someone else has developed, or about a service they are using.**

CASE STUDY: THORNHILL COMMUNITY GARDEN, CWMBRAN

Community groups in Thornhill, South Wales have been working together to develop a community garden to help make Thornhill a better, safer and more pleasant place for everyone to live. Local residents identified the need to improve the existing community centre and worked hard to transform a patch of derelict wasteground into a vibrant and precious community garden. BTCV Cymru has been working in the Thornhill estate for several years to encourage everyone to brighten up the estate. Nearly 40% of Thornhill's population is under the age of 19, and it is located in an area that lacks community resources and suffers from a high rate of crime and unemployment.

BTCV Cymru has been working with local community group, Thornhill 4 U to plan improvements to the community centre.

The area surrounding the centre was a wasteground, so an ambitious plan was developed to transform it into a community garden with something for everyone. Consultation events were held to ensure that everyone in the community had the chance to say what they wanted to see in the garden. Ideas included recycled furniture, seating and play areas, barbecue area and ceramic tiles bearing the names of groups and individuals.

The project reinforces the idea that quality of public spaces really does matter to people and sends out powerful messages about the state of the community.

Communities face so many barriers to practical action. From simply not knowing who to talk to for information, to lacking the skills and confidence to get the job done. So BTCV's approach has been straightforward – to provide an individually-tailored mix of support for each community. By listening closely to a community's aspirations and looking at the issues they face, we have been able to deliver support and practical help to those communities.

This project is an excellent example of how nature conservation can empower the community and enhance community pride. The longer term sustainability of the project has now been established. A weekly gardening club has been set up and has already attracted a wide range of members including people who are disabled and hearing-impaired..

Thanks to Prudential, which own the nearby Cwmbran Shopping Centre, £10,000 was offered from their Grass Roots programme to get the project underway. The community promptly swung into action and raised the remaining £10,500 through funding from the Communities Trust fund and Torfaen Community Halls Department.

- **Participation occurs when people are invited to be involved in planning and developing a project and can help shape it from the start. They may also be invited to help manage the project or service.**
- **Engagement can best be seen as the long-term result of participative working: people don't just turn up to specific events: they are involved for the long-term, they feel some ownership of the work that is being done and they can suggest new ideas etc.**

Participation takes place in many different ways, for example:
- People may participate in meetings about a new community centre because they want to know that it will meet their needs;
- People may participate in a planning inquiry because they want to stop a supermarket being built on fields near their home; and
- People may participate in a local project because they can see that it is likely to make their neighbourhood a better place to live.

CASE STUDY: GROWTH IN GROUNDS

Even smaller projects can provide valuable examples for further work. Growth in Grounds was developed by Conservation Volunteers Northern Ireland working with South Belfast primary schools to improve the schools' grounds.

The basic aim was to involve teachers, pupils and the local community in school ground development projects, but added to that was the desire to utilise those school grounds in the delivery of the National Curriculum by providing a more stimulating and exciting area for children to play, learn and grow. This also offered children and young people the opportunity to voice their opinions and actively participate in changing their environment for the better. The project has led to a big increase in parental and community interest in school grounds. Many of the children's fathers got actively involved in the work and helped deliver high quality end results.

The children now have an engaging and stimulating environment for education and play, and, equally importantly, they also have the right to have their say in how this environment looks and is

developed. Whenever they see their views being considered and their manpower required in carrying out the work, they are more likely to feel valued, and it makes them want to care for and look after their surroundings. The teachers of children directly involved in the GIG projects have reported better communication skills and behavioural improvements, and it is hoped that this will result in lower levels of vandalism, truancy and bullying in the long-term. The lessons learned from this project in terms of involving both parents and children in planning and implementing projects have informed further work that CVNI have done as part of EfA.

FROM CONSULTATION TO PARTICIPATION

One way of seeing the difference between Consultation and Participation is the 'ladder of participation' developed by an American, Sherry Arnstein in 1969. She suggested the differences between processes were based on the level of control which the participants have in any process.

The Ladder of Participation	
1 Citizen Control	
2 Delegated Power	Degree of citizen power
3 Partnership	
4 Placation	
5 Consultation	Degree of tokenism
6 Informing	
7 Therapy	Non participation
8 Manipulation	

Here consultation is represented as just one approach to participation – one which can help groups to work out what kind of involvement is being proposed. But it can make things seem too simple: different groups in the community may be at different levels on the ladder (they may have better contacts with the local council, and thus have more influence), and processes change and develop over time. There is often no need for a group to 'climb the ladder' if their needs are met in other ways.

We've started, so we'll finish...

Starting work in an area can bring a new group of people together. One of the best results that can be derived at the end of any project work is for the project worker or co-ordinator to leave those people as a confident group who can work and plan together and have a good idea of what they want to do next. This is explored in Part 2.6.

Even if they are already formed as a group, the work you are doing can help strengthen their ability to influence what goes on around them. Therefore, anyone responsible for any kind of short-term project should be thinking about how that work can support long-term development. It will help if you can occasionally bring together the people who are most actively involved in the work to talk about how it is developing. This time to evaluate (see Part 2.8) and to socialise is important for long-term development and can provide the opportunity to start discussing 'what happens next'. It's never too early to be thinking about the future.

ACTION POINT

If you are planning a new project think about and write out the specific areas where you wish to encourage public participation and consider the different ways in which you might get people involved in the various different tasks.

While housing development is on the increase in Ashford, Kent, councillors wanted to fend off urban sprawl by creating a sustainable woodland resource for local residents. A project that would allow them to experience the countryside on their doorstep for years to come.

Ashford Borough Council (ABC) identified Singleton Hill as a suitable area for its panoramic views over the town and surrounding countryside, and obtained it from Kent County Council – giving the Ashford Community Woodland project 50 hectares to work with and local residents green space to visit.

Set up in 1999, Ashford Community Woodland aimed to encourage a pro-active approach from local volunteers, enabling them to make substantial improvements to their own environment and enhance their health and well-being in the process.

BTCV was employed by ABC to co-ordinate the project, which received £21,000 initial funding from Rail Link Countryside Initiative and ABC itself. Using the Planning for Real technique, which creates 3-D models of development possibilities for a specific neighbourhood, the charity arranged a community centre exhibition in the hope of attracting positive input from visitors. The consultation resulted in the collection of 900 different ideas.

A steering group was formed from the most committed local participants to engage excluded groups and develop community capacity. Under the Group's supervision, an action plan for tackling the site was produced and the work was started. A community management plan was established in 2002 in order to address the project's chief objective of sustainability.

Part 2.3
Introducing diversity

'Everyone means everyone' is divided into two parts (Part 2.3 and Part 2.4). Both parts look at working with groups from diverse backgrounds, but this first part focuses on the idea of diversity in general, while the second part looks in greater detail at working with young people, disabled people, people with mental health problems, people from impoverished areas, and people from faith groups.

Same environments, different ethnic groups

We all live on the same planet! But although we share some of the same environment, our own local environment may differ enormously from that of someone just a few miles up the road. The quality of the environment, the problems associated with it and the actions that are needed to improve things can all be very different.

Just as our environments differ, so too do our communities. The UK is now one of the most culturally diverse countries on earth with many different faiths, ethnic groups, languages, interests and issues represented in the population. If we are serious about wanting to offer everyone in our communities the chance to be usefully and effectively involved, then we need to understand the problems we may encounter. Thinking about the diversity of any community is a good place to start.

Working with diversity

Diversity is a word used when talking about different ethnic groups, but it goes a lot further than that. Diversity is about the way people define the differences between themselves, and about how we can use those differences positively, benefit from them and celebrate them.

With those differences come needs and priorities, and those needs are likely to affect how people may participate in projects that you may be planning. Diverse groups within any locality may include:

- Young people;
- Older people;
- Ethnic minorities;
- Faith groups;
- Disabled people;
- Single parents;
- Gay men and lesbians;
- People suffering from poverty and deprivation;
- Those with mental health problems; and
- Refugees and asylum seekers.

All these groups of people can be seen as communities in their own right, co-existing within the 'community of communities' that can be found where they live and work. They make up the 'communities of identity' we discussed in Part 2.2 – the communities made up of people who belong to a specific group because they see it as an important part of their identity. It is very important to respect such communities. If you can get them involved they can be valuable, motivated and well-organised partners. People who are active in a particular faith group are one example, but there may well be others.

Working in partnership with a drama group from the Scottish Refugee Council Youth Project, the Positive Images project was a successful partnership that demonstrated how drama could work in connection with the environment. You can find out more about the Positive Images project in the case study on page 60.

The aim of BTCV Scotland's Positive Images project involvement was to link drama to the environment in a simple way. The drama group worked on a play which examined the issues of exclusion and loneliness, and challenged the audience to question their own attitudes towards what it meant to be a refugee. Using the play's central theme of a wishing tree, the group participated in a tree planting day on the banks of Loch Lomond, which also gave them the opportunity to film their play outdoors within a natural setting. The skills they learned were then transferred to schools throughout Glasgow as the group donated and planted a wishing tree for each school where they performed their play. This initiated discussion about what was important to them about their environment.

TAKE TIME TO THINK ABOUT:
What are the differences between communities of interest and communities of identity in any groups in your locality?

Equal Opportunities and diversity

Anyone who has worked with an organisation may well be aware of Equal Opportunities legislation. This is a range of laws that exists to ensure that no-one is discriminated against on grounds of ethnicity, faith, disability, age and other issues. The most important laws for this type of work are likely to be the Race Relations Act and the Disability Discrimination Act (see page 54). They set minimum standards – the requirements that must be adhered to in order to comply with the law. These are often seen in job advertisements where it will state that XYZ Company is (or 'is striving to become') an Equal Opportunities Employer.

This is an important issue for environmental groups, especially those with a history of predominantly white membership even when working in multi-ethnic areas. A good starting point for work on this field is to check the Equal Opportunities policy for your organisation (if you have one) and to examine how it is being applied and monitored. Equality of opportunity is an important starting point: if you don't get this right then it is likely that your attempts to work with diverse groups will fail.

But you don't just have to comply with the minimum requirements. Valuing Diversity is an increasingly popular way of working that moves on from simply checking that the Equal Opportunities regulations are being applied. Simply put, it is based on identifying and valuing the diversity of cultures and needs within the groups you work with and looking to work with those groups in the most appropriate ways to meet their needs.

In most of the UK, a further development has arisen with the 2002 amendment to the Race Relations Act (different legislation applies in Northern Ireland). This now gives local authorities and other major public bodies a specific duty to actively promote race equality, and sets out standards and targets that can help identify progress. You may be working in a much smaller organisation, but a number of environmental groups are now looking at how they can work in the spirit of this new duty and in so doing are broadening their outreach and appeal.

Starting to work with diverse communities

As you can see from the list on page 41, wherever you are there are communities with diverse needs and differing priorities. The most important first step towards working with diverse groups in any area is to be aware of them. This is where a good stakeholder analysis (see Part 2.2) comes in.

You can use this process to build better links with well-organised and visible groups by asking them to help identify the less obvious groups and communities. Some groups may be almost invisible until you go and look for them, because they are not well-organised or linked to public life. Walking round the area (see Part 2.1) and checking the cards and posters in libraries, surgeries and shops can help you see which small groups do meet and organise in the area. It may also be helpful to make contact with the social services workers in the local council who cover the area you are working in. Community and parish newsletters and local papers can also be good sources of information.

The second step is to focus on one of the most difficult groups: ourselves!

Like it or not we all have some preconceptions about other people and groups. You may find in your work that you need to challenge other people's preconceptions (about young people, old people, other races etc), but to do this, you also need to think about and work through your own.

There is support and assistance available on this. If you and your organisation are seeking to work with excluded minority groups then the staff involved ought to have (at the very least) basic awareness training. The local Council or the Council for Voluntary Service may be able to provide help and advice. If you do go on an equal opportunities awareness course, share the ideas and outcomes with other people you work with – this is an issue for the whole organisation.

However, it's not just about training. Overcoming preconceptions can take time. You can be more mindful about this in your day-to-day work by:

- Learning to listen closely: understand what's really happening in the area;
- Knowing the main interests of the groups you are working with;
- Being aware of your role, of who you are, and how you are perceived; and
- Being clear about the help that you can really provide.

Include everyone!

If your work focuses on communities and groups who are often left out, there are some people who you may be paying less attention to. These are people working with well-established community groups. It may be easy to say that these are the 'usual suspects' and that you are looking for new contacts and opinions, but these well-organised groups exist for some very good reasons, most importantly that many local people trust and respect them.

Even if people don't turn up to meetings of a tenants' group, it doesn't necessarily mean that they are a small unrepresentative clique: it may equally be that they are just getting on and doing what needs to be done. They may well have been voted in by local people, have a very good understanding of the local surroundings and may themselves also be keen to reach a new audience.

It is important to include active local groups. Keep a balance between the people who are keen to talk with you and the people who are unsure and unready. If there seem to be differences between these groups then try and set up some meetings where these can be discussed by both groups and if possible sorted out.

Women from different communities in Glasgow and from a variety of cultures have turning 'trash into art' in environmental activity workshops. The participants, predominantly from Afro-Caribbean and Asian origins, and representing a wide range of ages and physical abilities, have been brought together by their interest in art and a newly discovered role within their environment. The sessions enable them to explore their creativity and develop new skills.

The re-use of waste has obvious environmental benefits, but the workshops also achieve a genuine cross-cultural inclusiveness that is helping to build understanding between the communities. The workshops were established by a partnership between Network House and Meridian (two of Glasgow's major cultural centres) and BTCV Scotland.

Working with minority ethnic groups

Most of the points in this part apply to any minority group, whether it's disabled people or single parents. Good planning and good listening always matter. But work with minority ethnic groups can pose its own challenges and does need careful planning. Environmental groups have been seeking to develop this work for many years and there have been some major failures alongside the success stories.

Kent has a high number of refugees and asylum seekers and an alarmingly high proportion of these are unaccompanied minors. There was concern about the lack of support available to these vulnerable young people on arrival. Age and language barriers often make it impossible for these people to enter mainstream education.

A training course for young refugees and asylum seekers was set up to help provide practical solutions to help their integration within the local community. In the pilot phase, a group of teenage boys (including six Albanians and one Afghani) received training in a range of practical skills including how to use hand tools safely, stock fencing, hedge laying, access work (such as step creation), photography and IT.

Young people took part in practical sessions every Wednesday for 12 weeks. On many of these sessions, they worked alongside volunteers from the local community including other young people of school age. The success of the pilot has led to the development of a three-year project supported by the Camelot Foundation through their Transforming Lives scheme.

The project is a partnership between Kent County Council (which supplies advice and translators), The Kent High Weald Project (a countryside management project which runs the practical tasks) and BTCV (which developed and

delivers the training aspects of the project). In addition to the formal skills acquired by the young people, the project helps to introduce them to the new surroundings that they find themselves in, provides opportunities to work alongside members of the host community and reduces their feeling of isolation. It also gives them the opportunity to practice their English, and a space to chat through personal issues in an informal setting.

The participants themselves provide clear evidence that the project is working. Some young people who have now left the centre have asked if they can continue to take part in the weekly sessions, others have asked if they can develop land at the centre to grow their own vegetables on the site.

Staff at the reception centre confirmed that the young people have benefited from the experience and that participants often had their best night's sleep after the day's practical work.

The size and composition of minority ethnic communities in any area varies enormously. In some rural areas minority ethnic groups may represent only one or two per cent of the population; in other, more urban areas, so called 'ethnic minorities' may well be majorities. Where there is a substantial population, then planning carefully to involve these communities should be a priority. There is some history to deal with: some groups have in the past directly accused environmental groups of being for 'whites only': this kind of myth and attitude needs to be tackled by showing that it simply isn't true.

This is ever more important as diversity in the UK continues to increase. London is now believed to be the most diverse city in the world, with more languages spoken there than anywhere else. Many UK cities and urban areas include large well-established minority ethnic groups, and there are new smaller communities who may be less organised and have less understanding of local issues.

Success starts with good planning. Find out exactly which ethnic minorities are living in the area and if any organisations represent their interests. Many are well-organised with strong community networks. Faiths play a strong part in the lives of many ethnic minorities (but by no means all) and the local mosque, church or synagogue may have useful ideas and information. If you are at all unsure who to contact first then start by asking other voluntary networks, the Council, or your local Race Equality Council or Partnership for advice. When you're doing local survey work, remember that it's not just about skin colour: many minority ethnic groups, such as Bosnians, Armenians, Travellers and others are white.

Identify the communities and seek first to understand their priorities. They may be newly arrived refugees from war zones or they may be part of a community that has been here for hundreds of years. Try and find a few individuals who will spend time with you explaining these matters. Learn about and understand key cultural issues. These may well affect the ways you work (Orthodox Jews, for example, may not want to support project work on

CASE STUDY: HILLSIDE HERBS, DUDLEY

Hillside Herbs is a Community Enterprise project growing herbs and vegetables in Dudley in the West Midlands. It was set up in 2000 with support form a range of bodies including BTCV and the National Lottery. The activities are designed to be open to a wide range of people in a run-down area, including 16–19 year olds, SureStart parents (with pre-school age children), people on community punishment orders and young offenders and people with disabilities. The project provides a range of positive outcomes. Vandalism has fallen as the local young people have become involved. Some have joined training courses leading to NVQ and C&G Horticulture Skills. The work also provides a healthy lifestyle and eating opportunities for the local community with locally produced fresh organic food. The success of the project was shown when they won medals and a cup for 'Best in Show' at the regional West Midlands Network Flower Show run by Cultivations an organisation, which promotes therapeutic horticulture.

The organisers point out how the project has enhanced the local environment and improved employment prospects. As a result of exercise and healthy eating, there has been a marked improvement in community health. The integration with the local community is shown by the fact that the project base is now used as a meeting point for councillors surgeries and a neighbourhood watch group.

the Sabbath (Saturday), and you may need to provide prayer rooms for Muslims).

This is where hands-on local project work can be important and useful. It's easy to understand and, if you plan it well, easy to do and get involved in. Setting up a small local project can be a valuable way to build a better understanding and to begin moving towards greater long-term involvement. An initial discussion with interested people may be based partly on your ideas but should also be open to their ideas and proposals.

Food growing has been a common way to start joint working. Many communities want the fresh vegetables, herbs and fruits that may not be easily

available in local shops, and people may also have skills in gardening and farming. There are many successful projects working with ethnic minorities on these issues. Your local Food Links project (www.localfoodworks.org) or City Farm (www.farmgarden.org.uk) may be able to point in the direction of existing projects that might inspire people. But don't assume that everyone will be interested. They may be more concerned about unsafe open spaces in the area or lack of activities for young people.

Language is often an issue. This is more important in some cultures than others, and is often a major factor if you are hoping to work with older people or women. The best way forward is to get a few people from the particular ethnic community involved as early as possible and get them to help with day-to-day interpretation.

Many groups have started by translating information and leaflets. Your local Council or Race Equality Council (REC) can probably assist with this; be sure to build in the time and money for this to happen in your project. This may well raise interest, but be aware that people may then turn up for project work expecting someone to be there who can speak the language. This has caused major problems on a few occasions!

WORKING WITH TRAVELLERS
Travellers are among the most excluded minority groups in the UK, and are one of the biggest victims of discrimination. Often the sites they are offered are in desperate need of

CASE STUDY: THE BELFAST TRAVELLERS SUPPORT GROUP

There are approximately 1,400 members of the Travelling community in Northern Ireland. Surveys suggest they may be the most marginalised of the minority communities in the province. Conservation Volunteers Northern Ireland and the Belfast Travellers Support Group have worked to engage young people from the Travelling community in environmental activities. They have worked at the after schools facility at one of the Belfast Travellers sites and groups of young people have planted wildflowers, strawberries, herbs and vegetables.

improvement. **If you have the opportunity or need to start working with Travellers then do your homework carefully first. Find an experienced advisor from another environmental group or contact your local social services department. The National Gypsy Council (01928 723138) can also provide advice.**

Refugees and asylum seekers are often special cases: they may be the most deprived people in any community. They are likely to have been forced to leave their homes and have little say in the community they have arrived in, often being housed in the neighbourhoods that are least popular with local people.

In this situation it is no surprise to discover that they may not be clear on what they can do locally, but that does not mean that they don't have the skills and resourcefulness to improve their lives. If you are working in an area with a sizeable refugee population then a project with them may produce some very positive results. It is important to work through existing support agencies to see what kind of projects may meet their needs.

Don't ever treat minority ethnic groups as just that. Any group of people will have concerns, and theirs may not relate to their ethnicity. Their concerns may be partly about that, but could also relate to the fact that they are women or older people or are dog-walkers (or all of these things!). It's also important to be aware that minority ethnic communities are as different from one

another as any other community group is to its neighbours. Just because something works well with one group we shouldn't assume it can be easily replicated elsewhere.

Part 2.4
Everyone means everyone!

Same environments, different people

This part looks at the many other diverse communities that you will encounter in local project work. See the list on page 40 to remind yourself whom these may include.

Young people

Anyone who has worked with local communities will know how, all too often, young people are blamed for just about everything that is seen to be wrong in an area, be it litter, graffiti, vandalism or noise. To make matters worse, those doing the blaming are often the older people within the community, which encourages social divisions.

Many of the problems are associated with fear, especially fear of crime. While this is often seen as an issue for older people, there is plenty of research that shows that young people are also fearful too, and they are certainly most likely to be victims of crimes such as mugging.

The purpose of local project work is not to allocate blame, but to make things better in the long term. This means first asking why the problems are so bad in any area (and also exactly what the problems are, and how bad they really are).

Involving local young people in local action does help. As well as being 'something to do', it can also provide young people with skills in everything from teamwork to using tools, and may also involve project planning, publicity and fundraising.

As well as youth projects, BTCV training programmes and short courses (www.btcv.org/training) offer accredited training leading to qualifications such as NVQs. There is also plenty of evidence to show that involving young people in practical work, such as mural painting, tree planting or similar projects, leads to less vandalism of the completed projects, sometimes with the people who worked on the project acting as its guardians.

Youth work in the environment can vary enormously, not least because of age differences. Work with young children may mostly be done through schools. Developing school projects and gardens can be a good way to build a permanent resource for a school. While young children are often very keen to get involved in this work, interest in the environment tends to drop off sharply at around the age of 12–14 as other concerns become more important.

Work with young people is more regulated than any other type of environmental or conservation work. Concerns over child abuse mean that anyone participating in youth work needs to be checked with the police. This is a routine process that can take several weeks to complete, so allow time for it in your plan.

With this in mind, under no circumstances should any group set up a project to work with local young people without getting advice and guidance from experienced and trained workers. See the section in Part 2.10 on risk assessment for more guidance here. Ideally there should be a trained youth worker

Glenmona, in West Belfast, is a residential unit for boys across Northern Ireland, many of whom have been excluded from mainstream education. It is located in an area of extreme poverty and the boys at the Care Unit have often experienced abuse in the past. Conservation Volunteers Northern Ireland (CVNI) became involved with Glenmona after approaching

them to help develop an area of neglected land into a wildlife garden for the local community.

The project was initially intended to be purely environmental, but it soon became obvious that the environmental backdrop was opening up the opportunity to achieve personal goals for the boys.

The project involved a wide variety of community groups including BTCV Green Gym, Belfast Conservation Action Team and volunteers taking part through the Employer Supported Volunteering Scheme. Links have also been forged with the local resident Traveller population in order to improve community relationships as a whole in the area. The boys taking part came from across Northern Ireland, which helps to break down cultural and religious boundaries.

Creating the wildlife garden helped the physical environment, but the benefits extended far beyond. It also helped the boys involved gain a perspective on their personal environment and acted as a springboard for personal development. Being involved in a project where they were valued and goals were achieved has meant that many of the boys felt appreciated for the first time. They also learned to communicate socially and work as a team. These

children have previously undergone very traumatic experiences, and this project has helped them with safe stepping stones towards rebuilding their futures with confidence, enabling them to express how they feel and providing a useful tool to develop life skills. The project gave the boys the chance to express themselves creatively and to learn environmental skills and gain knowledge. This has most notably been used by members of the group in working towards an NVQ in Horticulture. This nationally recognised qualification gives the boys a lasting legacy from the project, aside from the physical benefits of the wildlife garden.

The CVNI Project Officers working at Glenmona found that building trust with the boys was the most challenging and also the most rewarding aspect of the project: 'I can't tell you how personally rewarding it has been to have the opportunity to make a real difference to these children's lives. I would like to think that when they look back on their childhood we could have provided a genuine life-changing experience for them'. By understanding the background of the boys and by being open to getting less physical environmental work done than envisaged, the project has become one that reflects EfA's aims.

BTCV and Age Concern Dudley have set up a project for older people in Dudley. The Wildlife Gardening project helps older people create wildlife-friendly gardens and in the process, turn something that was a burden into a new interest. Age Concern in Dudley found themselves with many requests from older people who needed help to maintain their gardens. Although they were interested in gardening, many of the older people were unable to carry it out unaided. Lack of mobility, onset of age, lack of resources, or having no friends or family to help, can all contribute to neglected gardens.

As well as the environmental and conservation aims, the project helps to combat feelings of isolation among the elderly population by engaging them with young volunteers.

Local young people are encouraged to volunteer for the project. Young people befriend and mentor the residents, as well as undertake the gardening and conservation work. Their involvement promotes inter-generational contact. The young people are also given the opportunity to take something away from the project by gaining practical horticultural experience and free accredited training from BTCV.

The elderly residents gained an improved garden but also regained independence and so improve their quality of life. The improved gardens all helped eliminate trip hazards in the garden and increased activity and fitness. A well cared for garden also masks the fact that a potentially vulnerable older person lives at the house, reducing the fear of burglary or attack.

The young volunteers have been able to develop life skills such as communication, self-confidence, time-management and leadership. They also have access to training and practical experience in horticultural and conservation skills including NVQs in Environmental Conservation. The project helps to alter attitudes and preconceptions towards the older generation.

---

involved in both planning and delivery. There are plenty of guidance manuals and training courses available – see the appendix for more information.

The situation is different in Northern Ireland and new legislation will come into force in 2005. The NI Volunteer Development Agency (028 9023 6100 or www.volunteering_ni.org) can advise on work with young people and vulnerable adults.

Older people

Older people are often a huge and underused asset in any community. People who may have developed useful skills in their working life may be keen to help, if only someone asks. For example, one local group, suffering from serious financial disorganisation, took almost four months to discover a keen new activist was actually a retired accountant.

BTCV has been following a strategy of 'Expanding the Boundaries of Conservation Volunteering' in order to become even more socially diverse as an organisation. Work to involve more people with learning and physical disabilities and/or mental health issues has proved extremely successful. BTCV is one of the first environmental organisations in the country to receive accreditation by the Disability Rights Commission for our commitment to recruiting and retaining disabled staff and volunteers.

Working across London Boroughs, BTCV is offering adults with learning disabilities a real chance to develop their employment potential through accredited training in horticulture. The training is designed to provide essential support and guidance to promote life skills and personal development.

Work takes place in greenhouses and specially designed 'poly-tunnels' with a controlled environment to grow plants and seeds.

Backed by the Learning and Skills Council, this is the first time many of the students have had the chance to study for accredited education. In the past their learning disabilities have been viewed as obstacles too big to overcome. The results have been extremely positive. Over four years, 120 beneficiaries have successfully completed the NPTC Vocational Foundation Certificate in Horticulture and 44 have gone on to complete the higher-level Skills for Working Life Award. The Minister for Disabilities, Maria Eagle, has also publicly endorsed this work by opening a new poly-tunnel at Merton College back in May 2003.

The project's success has enabled it to expand to incorporate working with young people. In liaison with local secondary schools, a training programme has been put in place to promote 'taster courses' in Horticulture. These courses open up new possibilities in life and career choices and promote self-confidence amongst those taking part. A Work Placement Development Officer funding by the ESF and Learning Skills Council London South encourages the sustainability of the project and promotes the link of transferring the skills gained from the project to the workplace. As a result, several people have successfully gained work experience placements in local garden centres and hospices.

Like any other group, older people have special needs and concerns. Many may not like to attend planning meetings in the evening, and often like to finish their work during the day by 3pm so that they can go home on a bus before the buses load up with young people on their way home from school.

There are plenty of ways to engage older people: a local branch of Age Concern can point you to existing organisations which may be interested to work up a suitable project. The increase in sheltered housing offers new opportunities for building links with existing small well-defined communities.

One of the obvious benefits to older people of working on a practical project (just as it is a benefit for others as well) is the chance to meet people: it's important to build social time into longer-term projects. There's a further benefit that has only recently been assessed: practical action is good for people's health. BTCV Green Gym projects (see page 78) have proved to be popular with many older people, and specialist evaluation has shown improvements in fitness and mental health as well as weight loss.

Working with disabled people

Many local environmental projects already successfully involve people with disabilities. There are obvious projects such as raised flowerbeds that can be worked by people in wheelchairs, or scented gardens for visually-impaired people, but there are many other approaches and organisations such as RADAR and Thrive that can provide more advice.

It's also important to try to make as much of your work as accessible as possible. If you're working on a site or in an office try and ensure full access for those in wheelchairs and ask them the type of work that they would like to do. If you're starting any new project make sure that the venue for planning meetings with local people is accessible. If it is not, then it will be best to have the meeting somewhere else. Having a disabled person unable to access your venue is annoying (for them), embarrassing (for you), and against the law.

If you're working on a long-term project, there's more to work on disability issues than just 'can people get to the site'. Just as with the development of diversity strategies for work with ethnic minorities, so there has been a steady change in work with disabled people. The old 'individual approach' which saw disability as the result of an impairment or medical condition that affected a person, and which tended to see them portrayed as 'brave' people who had suffered a personal disaster, is now seen as unhelpful. The 'equality approach' sees disability differently and has been developed by disabled people themselves. It shows that what really disables people are barriers which arise when the majority of society fail to take account of the needs and aspirations of the significant minority who have impairments or medical conditions.

The approach suggests that we need to tackle the four 'P's:
- People and their attitudes to disabled individuals;
- Policies that make life difficult for those individuals;
- Practices (such as information provision) that may affect disabled people adversely; and
- Physical features of the places and buildings in which we live and work.

All these can create barriers which can exclude disabled people. All these are things that we can tackle, both in specific projects and in everyday working life.

Some key facts

- 4–5% of disabled people use a wheelchair (more would if their housing and environment were more accessible);
- One person in four will have at least one disabled person in their family or household;
- Two million people use a hearing aid; 420,000 are unable to use a voice telephone;
- 6.8 million people are involved as informal carers for disabled people; and
- There are 360,000 disabled children in the UK.

THE DISABILITY DISCRIMINATION ACT (DDA)

The Disability Discrimination Act (DDA) was passed in 1995 to end the discrimination that many disabled people face. It protects disabled people in:
- Employment;
- Access to goods, facilities and services;
- The management, buying or renting of land or property; and
- Education.

For service providers (eg businesses and organisations):
- Since December 1996 it has been unlawful to treat disabled people less favourably than other people for a reason related to their disability;
- Since October 1999 they have had to make reasonable adjustments for disabled people, such as providing extra help or making changes to the way they provide their services;
- From this year (2004) they have had to make reasonable adjustments to the physical

features of their premises to overcome physical barriers to access.

For education providers, new duties came into effect in September 2002. These require schools, colleges, universities, and providers of adult education and youth services to ensure that they do not discriminate against disabled people. The duty to provide auxiliary aids, through reasonable adjustment, came into force in September 2003. The Government and the Disability Rights Commission (DRC) has produced a number of Codes of Practice, explaining legal rights and requirements under the Disability Discrimination Act 1995. These Codes are practical guidance – particularly for disabled people, employers, service providers and education institutions – rather than definitive statements of the law.

More information can be found at the DRC website (www.drc-gb.org/index.asp). The DRC works towards 'A society where all disabled people can participate fully as equal citizens'.

Working with disabled people – the language barrier

Many people who are new to working with disabled people are worried about using insensitive language. We can unknowingly use language that may irritate people and that can cause concern and embarrassment, but a little forward planning can probably resolve potential mistakes.

Firstly, don't get hung up on this issue. This is not about 'political correctness' – it is simply about working with and relating to people as they would like you to. Being sensitive to language is a skill to acquire like any other and everyone makes mistakes. If you are going to work regularly with disabled people then some training will be very helpful, but a few general points might include:

- Think about people, not about categories (this is pretty straightforward: talk about someone who has epilepsy rather than an epileptic);
- Avoid using the term 'the disabled' – they are disabled people and people with different abilities; and
- Don't be judgemental – avoid preconceptions and treat people with disabilities as you would anyone else, offering assistance as they request it.

BEST PRACTICE
Forward planning isn't as difficult as it may sound. Greater London Action on Disability (GLAD) gave visitors the following information for a recent conference at the major QEII conference centre:

Access Details
Entrance: The footpath approach to the conference centre from Broad Sanctuary is cobbled – difficult for people who have certain impairments. However there is a smooth ramped entrance on the right hand side of the building (if you are facing the building).
Registration will be on the ground floor as you come in past the security. The conference will take place on the fourth floor.

Parking: There are spaces for Blue Badge holders at the front entrance of the centre. This area is cobbled. Entrance only via Storey's Gate (opposite Methodist Central Hall) and there is a security barrier (please book so we can inform security who will raise the barrier to let you in).

Dropping off by taxi/minibus, car: You should ask drivers to go through the security barrier to the main front entrance to drop you off. The entrance has a ramp to one side for wheelchair users etc. but has three steps (one shallow, two higher) painted yellow to main entrance doors.

Refreshments: There will be refreshments available in the St James's Suite area at the beginning of the day and in the morning and afternoon breaks and lunch will be available there too.

Toilets: These are available on the ground floor and fourth floor. However, wheelchair-accessible toilets are only the ground floor. Facing the front entrance one is on your left, two others – walk between the six lifts, through the swing doors and two are on the right.

Cloakroom: On the ground floor to your left. There is a free cloakroom available on the day.

Sign Language Interpreters: These will be available on the day.

Quiet Room/Prayer Room: ask for details.

Smoking: The building is non-smoking, but you can smoke outside the main entrance.

Seating: Chairs firm with padded seats and backs some with arm rests (we can provide others on request in advance).

Lighting: There is fluorescent and natural lighting throughout.

Buses: The following routes go very close by and are (supposedly) fully accessible: 3, 11, 24, 53, 77a, 88, 148, 211, 453.

Underground: Westminster Underground is accessible. If lift is not working ask a member of staff for alternative. Access to the Circle and District Line is not accessible however, Jubilee Line is accessible though there is a gap between platform and tube but we are told you can get on the tube. St James's Park is also nearby but is not wheelchair accessible.

Therapy and mental health

Mental stress and mental health problems are very common, and affect individuals in every community. One in four people will experience some kind of mental health problem in the course of a year; one in six people will have depression at some point in their life; and one in 10 people are likely to have a 'disabling anxiety disorder' at some stage in their life. For manic depression and schizophrenia this figure is one in 100.

Horticultural and environmental work is now seen as a valuable form of therapy for many people with such problems. The national organisation Thrive (www.thrive.org.uk) links a wide range of such projects and can provide advice and contacts with existing projects. If mental health issues are likely to be a significant part of your work, then staff and key volunteers should undertake some training – any local mental health agency will be able to provide more information. If your project is working with vulnerable adults, then, as with young people, the project workers should be checked with the Criminal Records Bureau.

CASE STUDY: THE BLUE TEAM IN FERMANAGH

The Blue Team is a group of people facing a variety of health and social problems: people with learning disabilities, long-term unemployed, people suffering from depression and young offenders. Before the project started some of the group undertook limited occupational therapy by undertaking basic jobs in local factories, but when the factories closed they were at a loss of what to do. There were already problems in this rural area of Northern Ireland with high unemployment and high levels of depression and suicide. Fermanagh Conservation Action Team set up a conservation group to tackle these problems by undertaking maintenance work on high value conservation sites in Fermanagh's beautiful countryside.

From this has come an energetic self-sufficient group with a growing sense of community pride. They report increased skills and interest in the environment as well as improved mental and physical health. The physical outputs are also important: improved habitats and footpaths, helping increase visitor numbers to tourist attractions and improving disabled access to the countryside.

It was not easy at first. There were concerns in local communities about participants with learning difficulties. Those with little experience of disabled people did not think they were capable of doing much and initially they were offered very limited un-stimulating work to do. The group 'had to work harder than others to earn respect' but over time they went on to carry out more challenging and responsible projects. Now the staff running the project are fully experienced and the project works so well that there is a new problem: demand for their services and places on the project is higher than their capacity.

Other benefits have come through: some of the team have set up a can recycling enterprise, while several of the offenders taking part have reduced sentences.

Positive Futures works with young people with learning disabilities. For many people in this situation, coping with leaving the school and youth care environment is a major life challenge. The project's aim was to maximise the quality of this next phase of their lives by enabling them to positively respond to this challenge, gain independence, self esteem and confidence.

Conservation Volunteers Northern Ireland's Fermanagh Conservation Action Team is working with the Positive Futures Team, providing environmental and horticultural training and support with high levels of initial supervision. They have seen a steady increase in communication, independence and the life skills of the participants. Several have been supported to find employment in the environmental or horticultural sectors. The most recent phase of the project is the establishment of a food growing and healthy eating enterprise.

People in poverty

Despite recent improvements as more households have moved above the poverty line, it is still a hard fact of life for many urban and rural households. Their experiences of poverty vary widely and link to issues such as access to facilities, employment levels in the area, quality of housing and many more factors. For more information and the main resource bank for information and statistics visit www.poverty.org.uk.

The wide variations in how people experience poverty explain why many agencies talk about social exclusion, although many poorer households will point out that at the end of the day it's not having enough money that really matters.

Every area where there are significant levels of poverty (and there are many ways in which this is measured) has some form of anti-poverty programme, although in rural areas these may be much less obvious. If you are working in a deprived area, check with the local authority for information about local projects.

While the state of the environment may not be a prime concern for the poorest communities, surveys show that it is still an important issue. An unfriendly, unsafe environment is just one more problem, and is one that may put off businesses thinking of investing in an area.

It is often hard for environmental projects to build links with people and organisations in the poorer neighbourhoods. Some of the reasons for this are historical: environmental groups don't have much of a track record in this field, and anti-poverty workers have been known to adopt an attitude that suggests that 'the environment is all very well, but we've got real problems to deal with first'. The challenge for any environmental project is to show that it can offer genuinely useful and lasting improvements to these poorer communities.

If you are working in a poorer area, be aware that Neighbourhood Renewal programmes and Community Empowerment Networks may be able to fund and support practical improvement work.

Try to keep in mind a few priorities that will bring real benefits to the area:

● Wherever you can, make sure that what you are bringing economic benefits – shop locally, employ local staff, provide basic skills training, and create jobs where you can etc.;
● Build working relationships with anti-poverty programmes in the area – show them that what you're doing will help deliver their goals too; and
● Make sure your work helps deliver those improvements which are the most needed. That will help local people feel more positive about where they live.

BTCV in partnership with multi-cultural faith centres in Glasgow has engaged a group of young Asians on a faith based media project. After learning the skills of filmmaking, they are now using these skills to investigate the links between different faiths and the environment. The aim is then to engage people from the different faith communities, eg Sikh, Hindu, Jewish, Muslim and Buddhist, towards practical environmental activities reflecting their common beliefs.

Positive Images also worked on a project in partnership with the Muslim Network in Glasgow, on a week-long Summer School for 80 young Muslims at Mugdock Country Park. The younger group studied the biodiversity within the park using tree trails and treasure hunt activities. The older youths created short video clips answering questions geared at the environment and the Islamic faith. A tree was donated by the older youths in a symbolic gesture of giving something back to the Earth.

The Positive Images project illustrates that with innovative thinking and being responsive to communities' needs and interests, projects can continue beyond the EfA initiative.

Working with faith groups

Collectively, faith communities are the largest group within the voluntary and community sector. Yet they are sometimes overlooked when projects start looking to make links with local organisations.

Faith groups are usually easy to find in any community: a church, mosque, synagogue, meeting house etc can be a valuable first point of contact, and many have meetings around formal services at which community projects can be discussed. They may well act as gateways to other groups within the community. In some villages the church and the church hall may be the main community focus (but don't ignore other faiths once you've made links with the most obvious one!).

In areas with sizeable minority ethnic populations (see page 43), a faith meeting can be a good way to make links with those groups. Most faiths also have a strong conservation ethic within their key writings, such as the Bible or the Koran, and most have produced some kind of policy paper or review that sets out their position on national environmental issues. This can help stimulate discussion at a local level and a little bit of work on the internet will provide plenty of information.

There are already many local projects across the UK that link faith groups and environmental action; the 'EcoCongregation' project run by ENCAMS may be able to advise you. At the time of writing a national survey is under way, funded by WWF, which will provide more examples of what is going on.

CASE STUDY: ADAMSDOWN DIG & PLANT — DIGGING FOR THE FUTURE

The memorial garden at St German's Church in Adamsdown in Cardiff was in urgent need of care and attention when Chaela Carrell of BTCV first met some of the congregation. Most of the congregation were too elderly to do heavy digging, so they and the priest, Father Roy Dixon, started by seeking to build community involvement in order to give the garden a bit of makeover.

Together they have run a series of fun events to help get the flowerbeds into shape and replanted. All were well attended with people from three to 60 years old. They brought their enthusiasm and BTCV provided advice on using tools and then garden maintenance to help keep things looking good after the main work had been done. Support came from other partners and the Cardiff Housing Association, the Adamsdown Resource Centre, and Adamsdown Forum have all helped make the church grounds and attractive area that has improved the image of the whole community.

THE MAJOR UK FAITHS

There are many different faiths. The approximate breakdown at the last census (2001) looks like this:

Faith	No. of people
● Christian	42,079,000
C of E	
Catholic	
Presbyterian	
Methodist	
Baptist	
Quaker	
Others	
● Muslim	1,591,000
● Jewish	267,000
Orthodox	
Reformed	
● Hindu	559,000
● Sikh	336,000
● Buddhist	152,000
● Other religions including:	179,000
Ba'hai	
Jain	
Zoroastrian	

Meridian is a Glasgow based-group providing a Black and Ethnic Minority Women's Information and Resource Centre. It was one of the original partners and long standing partners of EfA in Glasgow. The Afro-Caribbean Women's Group is a cultural and heritage scheme for women and children, incorporating heritage and environmental activities.

The group has organised several countryside trips, starting with a trip to the Botanical Gardens. The women and children also made trips to Scotland's Highlands, Mugdock Park and participated in a clean-up at Luss, as well as trips to the countryside.

The group acts as a meeting point for people from Black and Minority Ethnic communities, while empowering women by giving them independence and responsibility and also opening up the environment for them. By using public transport for the trips the group not only use an environmentally-friendly form of transport, they also see how easy it is to access the rural areas around Glasgow. The informal setting also allows the women to improve their English and exchange cultural information, all helping to break down cross cultural boundaries and

help integration into the local community. Children also become actively involved in the environment when joining the trips and taking part in activities such as a mini-beast hunt.

The group learn about several environmental issues while on the trips including waste and recycling, identifying flora and fauna and green transport. But they also become more involved in and aware of their environment by actually visiting it. This hands-on approach gives the women a sense of connection to their local surroundings and so fosters a sense of belonging and integration. Once people realise they are part of their environment and have access to it they are more open to getting involved in voluntary projects. The women's group also demonstrated that beyond awareness of the environment, an emotional commitment between the members was established.

The group is now using multimedia as a tool to learn about the environment. The group is looking to integrate with other women from Meridian to develop a project looking at their heritage and how it links to Scotland.

Gay men and lesbians

Some minorities are not visible. Gay and lesbian people are as active on environmental issues as other people, but often don't identify themselves – partly because in the past some have reported some degree of hostility. In cities, with a large gay and lesbian population there will be strong networks and organisations linking people, many of whom may be interested to promote activities and get involved. BTCV provides opportunities for gay and lesbian conservation volunteers in London.

Women and single parents

Women, especially single mothers, are often very busy just looking after themselves and their children. They will almost certainly have interest in their surroundings: they may be concerned about green spaces and play spaces, about poor housing and about road safety and air pollution. They may well be aware of why recent developments do or don't work for them.

You may encounter initial difficulties working with people in this situation because they may be isolated and not active in community groups, but projects that have done so have been able to make real differences to their lives and their surroundings.

Ways to build links might include:
- Setting up joint projects with creches, nurseries, SureStart childcare centres, healthy living centres etc;
- Linking with parents of school age children through school, after school and holiday projects, and encouraging parents to help with these; and
- Offering training in relevant skills that may offer them ways into part-time work.

Creating opportunities for families to work together on projects which will enrich their lives, is one of the best ways of getting people interested in their own environment. The Prudential Grass Roots project in Reading has reached out to schoolchildren who have encouraged their parents to get involved, helping to raise awareness of the value of conservation to the wider community. Although it is generally considered an affluent town situated at a prime location along the busy M4 corridor, there are several areas within Reading suffering levels of deprivation which are above the national average. This project has helped to stimulate a creative approach to community action that has resulted in a significant contribution to the environment and sustainable development. The Grass Roots Programme, run by BTCV and funded by Prudential, worked with over 80 school children and their parents to create new environmental and educational features at three schools in Reading. Hands on practical guidance has been provided by BTCV. At Reading's GreenPark business complex, owned by Prudential, a nature trail has been designed as a fun and stimulating way to teach children about wildlife and the environment. As creative ideas evolved to become a practical reality, children and parents were inspired by this project. The nursery garden has been divided in two areas: the 'natural environment' and the 'urban environment'. Colourfully painted stepping-stones now provide a path to a wildflower meadow where special habitat piles have been built to attract insects and Buddleia bushes to tempt butterflies back into the area.

The urban environment developed an original 'road' feature in the grounds by adding a log train and parents created the designs for a pond mosaic, featuring Nemo the fish, so that children could enjoy a virtual underwater experience at break times.

A large, previous unused wooded area in the school grounds now has a fenced off area which has been transformed into an aquatic haven for frogs, toads and newts. BTCV staff worked with parents and children to create the pond and a raised vegetable bed for a gardening club. Wildflowers have been planted and the wood already existing in the area was used to create habitat piles for insects, amphibians and small mammals.

The GreenPark nature trail has a host of natural features and is home to a variety of plants, insects and wildlife. The creation of a nature trail has provided benefits to the wider community and schools who can now use it to learn more about the abundance of wildlife in an area close to their homes. Specially produced leaflets and an educational activity pack provide teachers with a ready made lesson plan which fits effortlessly into the Natural Curriculum.

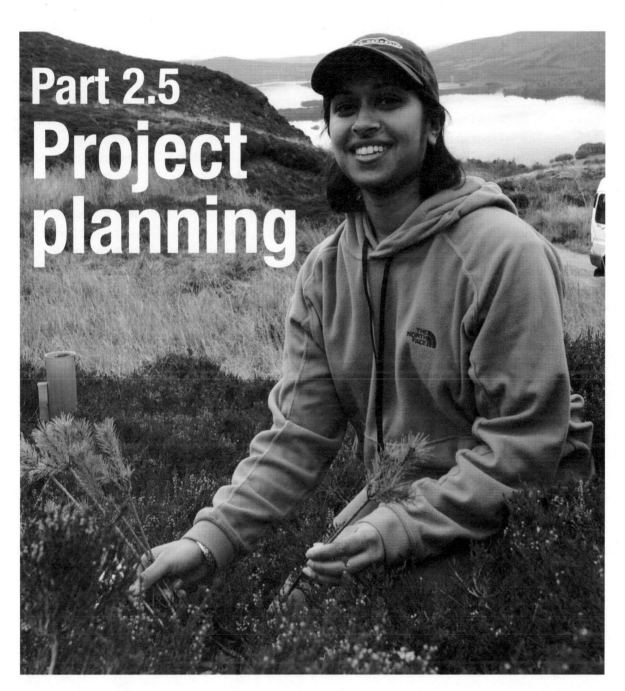

Part 2.5
Project planning

If the first part of your work is settling on an area or community in which to work, and the second part is engaging with that community, then the third part is being clear on exactly what you will do. To do this, you'll need to outline a clear plan and process that sets out what needs to be done, when and in what order, who will do it, and how you'll know you've succeeded.

This plan should, of course, be done before work starts, but developing such a plan, at least in outline, will also be an important part of your fundraising work. Anyone who is going to give you money will expect some clear evidence of what you intend to do with the money. Having a clear plan will help you draw up a good and realistic budget.

Starting to plan

Planning a project should start with three key questions:

- What do you actually want to see happen in the community?

This is your overall objective or outcome. It's isn't about something as simple as planting trees, organising training sessions or raising money: it's about what those activities contribute to. Your aim might be to produce long-term improvements in the quality of life in the area, or it might be to develop the skills and capacity of people and organisations in the area so that they can make improvements. Whatever it is, be clear about it and agree it with the community.

- What do you want to do to help achieve this objective?

This is your project goal. It may well be something as simple as organising a clean-up event in a park on a single afternoon, or it could be a three-year funded project with several staff. Whatever it is, it should be clear to you and others how it will help deliver that overall objective.

If you are clear on both these, then the rest of the planning process will be a lot more straightforward. It's mainly a matter of working out what needs to be done and in what order to meet the goal.

- What will it cost and can we afford it?

You may not be able to answer either part of this question at first (see Part 2.7 for more information), but keep this issue in mind as you go forward. There's no point in trying to plan for something that you will never ever be able to afford or fund.

Developing your plan

The nature of the plan will depend on what you are planning to do. It should also take account of what you have already committed to do. If your project is getting external funding then it is likely that you have already said, at least in outline, what you will do and when you will do it by.

This can be a useful base for any plan: indeed you will have to do some planning to work out how much money you need (see the part on fundraising). So an important first step is to review any existing commitments. If you've told your funders you are going to run 10 workshops for local people then making sure those happen is central to your planning.

The basic idea is simple: list the major outputs and then list the things you do to make each of those outputs happen (you should also list the things you need to do to make each of these smaller things happen). Be aware of the difference between your outputs and your long-term outcomes (see Part 2.8). Break the work down into single tasks: focus on one clear task at a time, examining exactly how it can be done, how long it will take and who will do it. This is also the time to be thinking about risks and problems – see Part 2.10 for information on risk assessment.

Depending on the level of planning you need to do, your plan can be less than a page of paper or it can be several pages long. It's better to go into too much detail at the planning process rather than run the risk of leaving out important information.

Once you have the key tasks you should, then set the dates by which things need to be done. Don't over-plan. There is no point in setting exact dates for things that will need to be done in eight months time, but you do need to know how those things relate to all the other deadlines and key dates.

If there are specific places where external advice or support is needed, then identify those and work out well in advance where you will get the help (and put

---

PRODUCING A LEAFLET – AN ACTION PLAN
You may well have some funding for publicity leaflets: an action plan for producing a leaflet might look like this:

Task	Member responsible:	Deadline:
Draft the leaflet text	Sally	5 July
Edit and agree the final text	Sally, Razia, Mike	10 July
Contact designer	Razia	7 July
Get final text to designer	Sally	11 July
Get quotes for printing	Mike	10 July
Agree design	Sally, Razia, Mike	15 July
Get final design to printer	Mike	17 July
Pick up leaflets	Mike	19 July

This may seem like 'micro-management', but if the people involved all know what they and others are doing, you have a greater chance of success. If new people are involved, then such a plan can help them to see where the work fits in with everything else they are doing. It will also become clear when different people need to work together and arrange to meet.

Leicester is a richly diverse city and the EfA team has worked to bring the different communities together through projects that link different faiths, different social backgrounds and cultures.

An initial project worked closely with three main groups: Gujarati Muslims, Gujarati Hindus and Sikhs. While the project crossed religious boundaries the groups shared similar backgrounds. The opportunity for these groups to engage with each other to discuss their environment proved very successful and a Rangoli garden was created.

Other projects have followed, including:
1. Staff helped the Braha Samaj Community Centre and BTCV to organise events for the Nauratri and Diwali Celebrations. Approximately 50 families attended every night for the duration of nine nights. The Nauratri evenings included worship, religious dancing and informal environmental awareness training. The Diwali celebrational event brought about 325 people together and also drew in several environmental groups.

2. In Braunstone (near Leicester), the EfA team worked in partnership with the first Asian mayor for the town to run an environmental Multicultural Day in March 2004. This celebration of diversity also highlighted the value of joint working by the voluntary and statutory sectors in Leicester and Leicestershire.

The project began in 2001 and issues around cross-cultural understanding have improved steadily, thanks to the determination of community volunteer officers. One worker said: 'The best by-product of our work is that many entrenched negative values and beliefs are gradually eroding. This is happening because our work gives people from all parts of the community a chance to get to understand each other while improving the environment. We have made great strides towards eradicating many of the "isms", such as racism, sexism, homophobia and islamophobia.'

this in the plan as an action point!). One area where such help may well be needed is planning what to do with a specific piece of land. What looks like an overgrown wasteland to some people may be an important wildlife site to others. If you are working on such a site then you will need a management plan: getting one of these developed is described in the next part.

One final point for your plan: use it as you draft it to spot the potential hold-ups (where 'we can't do

action 14 until we've done action 16') or mutual dependencies ('actions 8, 12 and 15 all link to action 4 and to each other') and to external deadlines ('we have to report to the funders about action 16 by 1 November, but the plan says we don't do this until mid-December'). Rearrange your plan to make these things fit as well as possible.

This is also the time to review the costs of the project. You should now have a much clearer idea about what the costs will be and so you can start to prepare your fund-raising work (which may need its own plan of action! – see Part 2.7)

In all this work remember one thing: a plan is only any good if it is shared and available to everyone who is involved in making it happen.

A management plan for your site

If your project is based on improving or developing a specific site then it is important to consider whether you need a management plan. This is a plan to set out how the proposed work will affect the environmental and amenity value of the site and to ensure that it is managed in such a way that the biodiversity will be maintained or improved.

Producing a management plan may well be an important part of the project itself. Developing such a plan can be a very good way to get local people to learn more about the site and to appreciate its value. It is however a technical exercise and if you do not have the skills and experience to do this then you will need to get outside help.

It's not a difficult exercise on most sites. Most management plans use one of a range of 'standard' formats, and guidance is available on how to write one. Your local BTCV office can advise on this. Plans don't have to be long and formal as long as it is absolutely clear what is to be done. The key is to ensure that the right conservation work happens, and that the species on the site are understood and looked after when the work is being done.

To make sure that happens, you want a plan that everyone involved can understand, so keep it simple and clear. If there are technical parts, such as a list of species present on the site or ways that your plan links with the 'Local Biodiversity Action Plan' (probably developed by the local council) then make sure these are introduced with some clear text.

The action points in the plan are crucial: it should be very clear who is going to do what and when they will do it. If external workers are coming in, their role needs to be clear and someone needs to be responsible for briefing and supervising them.

If you are writing the plan (with or without outside help) then there is a set of standard questions you need to ask. Do this with the group of most active people and it can be a useful learning experience: you will find out which questions you can answer yourselves, and which you need help with. It should also become clear when and where you might need external help with some of the work.

Any management plan should ask and try to answer these questions:
- What is the history of this site?;
- What habitats are present now?;
- What wildlife uses the site?;
- Who uses the site?;
- What wildlife and habitats are most important to keep or improve?;
- When and how do you want people to use the site?;

- Are there conflicts between how people and wildlife want to use the site, and how can you best resolve these?; and
- Are there conflicts between how different groups of people want to use the site, and how can you best resolve these?

From plans to action

Once the plan, which may include your management plan is complete, then it should be put into action. Part of that transition is in making sure that everyone involved (not just the people who drew up the plan) understand it and what is proposed. Put some time aside to explain it to people, preferably before it is absolutely finalised, since they may spot things that have been left out.

Then, if it's not clear already, go through the plan and make sure it is entirely clear to everyone who does what and when it needs to be done by! If everyone is happy with the plan and understands their part in it, then your chances of having a successful project are much greater.

It may also be the case that your plan requires people to carry out work they've never done before. If you're going to plant trees, who is going to show people how to do this? And indeed, who knows where to get trees from? This is the point at which you may want to include in the plan some training for staff or volunteers. Don't imagine that you can bluff your way on important issues.

Lastly, there's one other important point: don't get too stuck on the plan! You need a clear plan, but you also need flexibility. If your evaluation suggests that it simply isn't working (see Part 2.8) then make some changes. If a major opportunity comes up to do something that everyone involved agrees is more useful and important but needs to be done now, don't stick with the original just for the sake of it. But do be very clear what changes you are making and why. Make those changes in consultation with the people who drew it up to ensure everyone knows what changes are proposed and why. In some cases you may want to review your objectives too. Can they still be achieved, perhaps in a different way?

Get Real was a holiday programme providing opportunities for young people to access new environments. Over the course of five weeks, a series of residential breaks were organised in Herefordshire and Worcestershire to engage young people from urban areas. Funding came from the Big Lottery Fund.

The objective of the holidays was to give young people the opportunity to get out of their normal daily routine, to enable them to experience new activities and to open their eyes to new environments. Over the five weeks, 86 young people aged 12 to 17 from across the West Midlands and many deprived inner city areas participated in the Get Real breaks. Activities included canoeing down the River Wye, feeding farm animals, fruit picking, building steps on an Iron Age fort, and horse riding.

The activities gave the young people a chance to develop many different skills. Their confidence grew as they tried new activities, such as horse riding, and spent time talking to new people and in some cases being away from home for the first time. They learned new practical skills such as how to read a map, willow weaving and, in some cases, how to ride a bike, and always left at the end of the week with a sense of achievement.

The weeks took place at the height of *Big Brother* mania, and some groups insisted on watching the reality TV series every night. The organisers used this theme and developed their own 'Big Brother house' where the group faced various challenges, which included doing the Hokey Cokey and cleaning 20 pairs of dirty boots. As one organiser said: 'We didn't get one complaint: they seemed keen to take on any chore. Popular culture can be useful at times!'

Part 2.6
All in a
day's work

Keeping up the momentum

Much of this guide so far has been about getting things going, looking at planning new projects, working with people and making sure everything you do is likely to work. This section looks beyond that at how you can ensure that the work you're doing with local people leads to genuine change in the long term.

It looks at three important areas:
- Capacity building – helping local people to be more effective;
- Forming a permanent group – ensuring that local people can work together for longer than the immediate project; and
- Community development – developing an integrated programme that will help communities change themselves and their surroundings.

It may be that the groups with whom you are working are already organised, but if they're not, then helping them get that way could be one of the most important outcomes of your work.

1. Capacity building

One way to help ensure that the work you are doing will continue to flourish in the future is to focus on 'capacity building'. Although this is a technical term, it means what it says: it is about helping people and organisations to develop new attitudes, skills and ways of working. By thinking in this way you can help increase their capacity to bring about change.

Ideally your work on capacity building should help everyone involved in the group's activities build skills and experience. This can also include funders and local council staff, but in their case you are only looking to build their capacity to work more effectively with local people.

The principles are pretty simple and many of the issues have been covered elsewhere in this book. You should:
- Work in a way that builds confidence, shares information, develops skills and encourages initiative; and
- Consider and apply equal opportunities principles at all stages of organisation and activity.

These are easy to say, and harder to do, but if you get into the habit of working in ways that build the skills of others, then you will be laying the foundations of a strong and effective organisation.

There are plenty of guides and books on this, but some simple pointers include:
- Encouraging people to do regular tasks themselves by showing them what to do and explaining why it needs to be done;
- Setting aside some time for informal discussion about how people feel the work is going, noting down any concerns and organising some on-the-job exercises that may help people gain confidence in the areas where they feel weak;
- Asking volunteers and those actively involved to do a simple audit of the things they think they are good at and things they need to know more about. Follow this up with training to help fill the gaps;

CASE STUDY: YOUNG OFFENDERS IN WAKEFIELD

The Wakefield Youth Offending Team and the Youth Restorative Justice programme are working with BTCV to help transform the lives of many young offenders in the area and to help them build a better future. Locking up young criminals is often seen as the solution to youth crime, but in fact, most young people sent to prison go on to commit more crimes when they are released. Community-based projects such as this help to stop young people committing crime by tackling the causes of their offending and helping them integrate into society.

The project provides repeat young offenders aged between 13 and 17 years with an opportunity to take part in practical conservation activities as well as essential support. Some of the offenders are places under intensive supervision orders, which means that they have to be accompanied at all times by staff from Wakefield Youth Offending team. They are all under 'reparation orders', which means that they have been convicted by the courts and instead of going to jail, they have to fulfil a quota of community service as part of their rehabilitation scheme. Benefits of this approach include reduced offending, drug dependency, improved their health and general mental well-being. There are also wider benefits to the local community, which include improving the quality of green space in the Wakefield area. The group is currently working on an area of land which will eventually be transformed into a nature reserve.

Reparation orders are available for any juvenile (10–17 years old) who has been convicted of an offence. The idea is to prevent the young offender from committing further offences by confronting them with the consequences of their criminal behaviour, and allowing them to make some amends. This project provides 'diversionary activities' in the form of practical conservation work to prevent re-offending. This activity is also seen as an alternative punishment (of a community service type) than going to jail and meets current governmental policy.

The project is now funded by the Neighbourhood Renewal Fund. It has been shown to be a vital part of the offenders' rehabilitation programme. BTCV is also building links on this work with substance abuse charities and has established partnerships with mental health charities. These groups work with people who benefit from environmental activities through increased general mental well-being and physical fitness. Many of the young offenders suffer from mental illness and Green Gym activities have demonstrated the impact of such activity on the improvement of health and well-being.

- Using the evaluation tools in Part 2.8. so that everyone in the group has a chance to sit down and talk with each other about the successes and the problems;
- Sharing your knowledge as much as possible: don't be a know-all but make sure that ideas and information do get passed on to others;
- Organising an annual group 'stock take' or development session; and
- Making sure that people know what training is available locally and encourage them to attend courses if they are interested.

2. Forming a permanent group

The aim is to get people to think not as individuals, but as a group. This takes time: people need to develop respect and trust for one another and to know who other people are and what they think.

If the work you are doing is moving towards its end and some people are clearly keen and interested, then a good step is to call a special meeting to discuss and work out 'what shall we do next'. It makes sense to discuss this with three or four other people who may be prepared to act as a core group to help take things forward.

A first step may be to try and agree some common purpose. It's fairly likely that people won't be working with you just in order to make one specific change: they've more likely become involved because they want to see real improvements in their neighbourhood. A simple facilitated discussion with someone, perhaps yourself, recording all the key points, should help show people that they do share some common vision. It is important to try and write it down: aim to come up with and agree a simple phrase such as:

We are people living in the Sandy Lane neighbourhood, and we want to work together in order to improve the quality of life for everyone in this area.

That's a simple start: if that's what you want to do, then the second step is to agree your aims – the things you want to do in order to achieve your purpose. These might be to tackle fly-tipping, to

The Enviro Kids group includes children from the ages of 8–16, all from the local Chinese community. The group was originally set up by BTCV through partnership with the Meridian Centre for Black and Minority Ethnic Communities in Glasgow. The group uses conservation as a way of involving the children in their environment. They participate in tree planting, guided walks, and tree identification classes. They are also given cameras and asked to take pictures that encapsulate what they think of as the environment and anything else they see that is interesting. This gives the children a sense of empowerment and responsibility, a direct involvement in the environment and a reason to ask themselves what 'the environment' is.

The children have a chance to see a different environment from their urban surroundings, and by making the activities conservation based, they are able to engage with the environment and to begin to feel ownership and a sense of belonging. The children also make social contacts, helping to inspire confidence.

This project predominantly consists of one ethnic group because they had already formed as a holiday club. However, like all the projects now developed, the emphasis is on integration with project days being open to all.

provide better facilities for young people, to improve the biodiversity, to make sure the council delivers local services well, and so on.

The third step is to consider how you will do things: the specific actions and projects that make the group a real organisation.

Forming the group

If you have agreed on the priorities, then you're well on the way, but there will come a point where someone should raise the issue: 'we need to get organised as a group'.

It's worth formally getting the agreement on this by getting all or most of those present to accept that: 'if we're going to do the kinds of things we've talked about, then we need to be organised'. This is important because it may help to lessen the bureaucracy involved in becoming a formal organisation. Plus, if you get the commitment at the start, then people are much more likely to stay involved through the initial formalities.

One good way to get things moving is to choose a name. Is it an action group? A resident's association? A conservation group? A local forum? There are all sorts of possibilities. What you call your group will help define how it is seen by other people. A catchy name can help, as can some good initials (but if you are based somewhere like the Sandy Lane neighbourhood mentioned above, think hard before agreeing on the Sandy Lane Action Group!).

The best way to help organise your groups is to get help locally. Your local Council for Voluntary Service (CVS; or VDA in Northern Ireland) will almost certainly be able to provide help: this is basically what they are for! They can provide a draft of a constitution (needed to set up a bank account) or a set of rules. They can also help you answer questions such as: Which is more suitable for our group: registering as an unincorporated association, a trust or an incorporated company?

- Unincorporated association
  This is perhaps the simplest local structure: it simply means that a group of people have agreed to come together for a particular purpose. The group can decide how it operates and liability for problems usually rests with members. However, such an association has no legal identity and it cannot own property or employ people.

- Trust
  This is a simple not-for-profit body where the elected trustees, usually seen as 'the committee' are responsible for the work of the group and the purposes of the group are set out in a 'trust deed'. This is a good structure if you are going to own a piece of land or some other type of property.

- Incorporated company
  This is in effect a business and can do the things that any business can do – employ people, trade and so on. The liability of the elected people (directors rather than trustees) is often limited so that they are not responsible if there is a financial disaster (thus you see many 'limited companies').

Any of these structures can become a charity. However, becoming a charity is quite a complex process and you should definitely get help. BTCV publishes a charity registration pack which has all you need to help you become a charity (available through the BTCV on-line shop). It will help with raising money, but it requires more administration. It often makes sense not to rush in to forming a charity when you set up a group, but to plan for it. A charity will probably need a more detailed constitution than an unincorporated association, so if you think that you may wish to become a charity, it may make sense to set yourselves up as a trust from the start.

The group will also need officers, who normally form a committee to take routine decisions in between the larger meetings and manage the funds etc. There will need to be a Chair (who chairs the meetings and is normally the 'spokesperson' for the group), a Secretary (responsible for legal matters and ensuring records are kept), and a Treasurer (responsible for the money).

Launching your group

You and your colleagues may already be an active group of people, but it's often good to let people know when you are formally launching yourselves as a group. The local press may be interested, and you may find that some people are more ready to get involved when they can see more clearly what they are joining.

Being a group is also useful if you are seeking assistance or are looking to work with other bodies, such as the local council or BTCV, who can provide advice and assistance. They will be much clearer about who they are helping, if you are for example, the Southfields Neighbourhood Action Group, rather than simply a group of people who happen to live in the area.

A launch is also a good opportunity for a celebration, so if you've done the paperwork and have a core of members, then hold a launch meeting. If you've completed a project then you can talk about that. It may also be a good opportunity to consult with local people about ideas for the future. You may also wish to invite local councillors, other local organisations, the press. Don't have too much formal speaking, allow time for discussion and also allow time for socialising: people ultimately join groups to enjoy themselves!

3. Community development

Community development is about structured approaches to work with communities. At one level it is a professional discipline with skills and qualifications, but it's also a good description of what good community project workers are doing much of the time. It's an area where experience can be as valuable as skills, but having both is often the best way to be successful.

Sometimes 'working with communities' does not mean much more than offering some consultation. This may be all you need to do if you are running a one-off project, but it is unlikely to help change the neighbourhood in the long term. Successful work

CASE STUDY: NEWHAM GREEN GYM

The Newham Green Gym is one of over 50 across the UK. Like the others, it offers volunteers the chance to carry out worthwhile practical conservation work while enjoying the health benefits of tailored exercise programmes and 'working out' in the open air. Unlike many of the others, it is working in a run-down inner-city area, and developed when the Primary Care Trust covering the London Borough of Newham saw the results of Green Gym and approached BTCV to establish one in their area.

The project is now engaging people who lead an inactive lifestyle, including those who experience isolation and mental and physical health problems. The Green Gym links practical conservation activities with essential warm-up and cool-down exercises to prevent muscle strain. The sessions combine the benefits from outdoor conservation tasks with upper and lower limb exercises and follow key health and safety criteria. Practical activities include digging, preparing the ground, planting native trees and shrubs, laying paths, creating a bog garden.

Members have carried out this practical conservation work in a nature reserve and tree nursery site at a local park, but they have now added a remarkable core project. They are now working to transform a derelict and neglected garden at the Independent Newham Users Forum (INUF). INUF is an independent mental health survivor-led and run organisation. It enables those with mental health problems to be involved in the planning, development, monitoring and evaluation of the mental health services they receive in Newham and East London.

The hidden garden, which is close to a busy main road and the Stratford shopping centre in Newham, is a precious green space in a largely urban environment. It has become a focus of conservation activity and provides numerous benefits for the local community. The Director of INUF has been delighted: 'For the last two years it had been a grim, derelict place that no-one wanted to sit in or look at. Now the garden at Ithaca House is becoming a wonderful safe haven of peace and enjoyment for all our members and visitors to the building.'

The Green Gym in Newham has opened up conservation volunteering to a new audience. Local health practitioners now recommend Green Gym sessions to their patients because of their proven ability in improving fitness, relieving stress and increasing feelings of well-being.

with communities takes more time, and needs both professionals and the community to learn to trust each other and to understand what is really needed in the area. A well-planned piece of work may indeed just be a specific project, but ideally it should do more than simply make that project happen. The community should end up with new skills and ideas: that's at the core of community development.

Community development is a bit like sustainable development: there are many definitions of it and people tend to focus on the bits that match their interests. But there are some widely used key points: these come from the Community Development Exchange (www.cdx.org.uk):

- Community development is crucially concerned with the issues of powerlessness and disadvantage: as such it should involve all members of society, and offers a practice that is part of a process of social change.
- Community development is about the active involvement of people in the issues that affect their lives. It is a process based on the sharing of power, skills, knowledge and experience.
- Community development takes place both in neighbourhoods and within communities of interest, as people identify what is relevant to them.
- The community development process is collective, but the experience of the process enhances the integrity, skills, knowledge and experience, as well

as brings equality of power, for each individual who is involved.
- Community development is about developing the power, skills, knowledge and experience of people as individuals and in groups, thus enabling them to undertake initiatives of their own to combat social, economic, political and environmental problems, and enabling them to fully participate in a truly democratic process.

The common word here is 'power'. Community development helps individuals develop the power to take their own decisions and change their own lives. Helping communities take power is not always easy – indeed many community groups may be happy simply doing what they're doing. But many do want to see long-term change: you may not be able to help them get a new school or health centre, but the skills and experience that they get from working on a local project may be very valuable in such longer-term objectives.

A wide variety of techniques and methods can be used to engage people as part of community development. The Community Development Foundation publishes a range of guides and books: their website (www.cdf.org.uk) has more information. There are also many training courses that range from one-day events focused around a single technique to long courses leading to professional and academic qualifications.

The Grass Roots project, run by BTCV and funded by Prudential, has provided valuable support to the local community of Manningham; an area that traditionally lacks green space. BTCV worked in partnership with The Bradford Community Environment Project (BCEP) to turn derelict land into a prized community garden, helping to change the image of an urban sprawl. The Grass Roots programme has also enabled the Scotchman Road Asian Grower's Group to develop a community allotments project.

Manningham was previously an area of Bradford scarred by deprivation and unrest. It hit the headlines in 2001 when it became the epicentre of violence resulting in Britain's worst racial tension for decades. Recently, support from statutory bodies and other organisations has helped to regenerate the area and paint a brighter future.

St Mary's Community Garden was once a dangerous fly-tipped area at the back of a row of terraced housing and despite repeated clean-ups by the local council and residents, the area presented a serious health risk. Frustrated local residents took action through the St Mary's Residential Association, and approached the consortium of partners, local community action group, BCEP, Prudential and BTCV. Their aim was to transform the site from a threatening liability to an emblem of neighbourly spirit, named St Mary's Community Garden. They also wanted to develop an allotment site in the local area. Other organisations involved in the scheme included the Scotchman Road Asian Women's Growers Group, four local schools, SureStart Manningham and Girlington SRB and the nearby Prudential-owned Kirkgate Shopping Centre.

Using nature conservation as a tool, St Mary's Community Garden and Scotchman Road allotments project has helped to empower local residents. The unsafe site was cleared of fly-tipped rubbish and stone walls were restored in order to deter further dumping. Litter-picking groups were organised, paths and raised beds were built for the purposes of access and inclusion, and plots for organic fruits and vegetables were developed. An area of green space was created where parents could let their children play safely on vandal-proof equipment, and an ownership of the local environment was stimulated in the neighbours who took part. Further to amending the principal site, the scheme also helped to expand the community allotments used by the Asian Women Growers Group, creating two new cultivation plots and improving prospects for permanent planting.

The project has provided an accessible, rich and varied resource for the whole community, used by schools, conservationists and lifelong learners.

Catherine Riley, Manager of the Kirkgate Shopping Centre, praised the site: 'This remarkable transformation is a credit to both the local residents and a number of colleagues here at the centre. We are very proud to have been able to play our part in this scheme, and look forward to seeing the community enjoy the garden.' Naweed Hussain, Chair of the St Mary's Residents' Association, was also pleased with what the community has created: 'This site has been a real eye-sore for years now. We kept clearing it, but it only got tipped on again. The result of all our work has shown people this area is used and cared for and that it's not an area for tipping anymore.'

Above: before and after

St Mary's Community Garden has received the Green Pennant Award, a national award run by the Civic Trust that recognises high quality green spaces in England and Wales that are managed by voluntary and community groups.

Part 2.7
Paying
for it all

Fundraising and budgeting

If you are running a small project where people are simply interested in doing small-scale improvements and contributing the necessary time and equipment (right down to rubbish sacks), then you may well be able to do it for no money at all. But most projects have to pay for something (from rubbish sacks and cups of tea up to full-time staff and offices) and the money to pay for things has to come from somewhere.

This short section gives you an overview of what fundraising is about. To do this well you need training and support. BTCV provides training courses (www.btcv.org/training) and your local BTCV office or local Council for Voluntary Service will be able to offer you both books and guides.

Much of the information in this section is derived from existing BTCV materials. If you aim to run projects and raise money then those materials are important and you should certainly get training from more experienced people. A good fundraising course can transform how you raise money, and in turn transform your project.

Taking care of business

Local groups spend money on all sorts of things. The wages, the office, the hire of a van are all obvious: smaller sums for room hire, photocopying, tea and coffee are less noticeable but are important too.

Most community groups start small. If you are trying to run any kind of project you will need to know:
- How much money you need;
- How much money you have raised;
- How much money you have at any point; and
- What the money has all been spent on.

If you're going to raise money you will need to have somewhere to keep it, and you will need to convince those who might fund you that your group is competent. If you are part of a voluntary group that is going to operate efficiently, you need financial accounts and a treasurer to look after the 'books'. It may be that if you are employing staff then you will have a financial officer, but that person should be supervised by a treasurer who is a member of the group.

Finding a good treasurer is an important place to start. If you are running a project you will need to trust this person and they may make the group's life a lot easier. So look for someone who has some experience of handling money. For example, a retired bookkeeper often may make an excellent treasurer for a community group: if you have someone who is happy to be treasurer but who has no experience then arrange for them to have some training.

WHAT DOES A TREASURER DO?
The duties of a treasurer in a small group are fairly straightforward. They are to:
- **Keep a record of income and expenditure;**

- Make sure that important payments such as insurance are made on time;
- Deal with matters relating to the bank or building society account;
- Work with the group's officers and staff to ensure that money is coming in and that the group stays in credit;
- Produce a regular financial update for meetings;
- Produce an annual financial report; and
- Keeps good records and accounts.

Getting your funds organised

One of the first things a treasurer should do is to set up a bank or building society account. Several of them offer a 'clubs and societies' account which is a low-cost way to run an account. It is worth asking your own bank manager for advice. If you have been with the bank for several years, she or he even be able to help sort you out a low or no charge account. You should stress that you will not be looking for any form of overdraft. Seek advice from other banks as well before agreeing anything.

Group accounts will normally need more than one signature. It is sensible to have a system where any two out of four nominated signatories are able to sign a cheque. This means that money can be spent when one or two key people are away, but it also provides security for your group.

Regular bank statements can be a valuable way of checking both how much money you have and whether your accounts are in order. Some banks supply monthly statements as a matter of course, while others may ask you to specify what you want The records for that account should link to the group's own accounts and as the group grows so the accounts should too. There will be a range of cost and expenditure headings, and you will need to know how much is being spent on each, especially if you have set a budget for that expenditure.

It is also important that the rest of the group understand the role of the treasurer and the need for accurate accounts. If a small group gets a large grant for the first time then people may think 'we're in the money' and make some bad decisions or even try and spend the money without authorisation or agreement. If people are to spend money make sure it is agreed by the group or whatever body is co-ordinating the project you are running. Large sums should be specifically agreed, and you may wish to set a limit on how much the coordinator or worker may spend without consulting more widely.

For small sums try and get people to spend the money first, get receipts and then claim it back. It is important that your treasurer is very prompt in meeting such claims, and equally important that everyone get receipts for expenditure.

Keeping good records is not very exciting. Too often it ends up near the bottom of a list of priorities. Make sure this does not happen to your finances. Keep records of all income and expenditure as soon as it comes in or goes out. The treasurer and group leader should meet regularly to make sure that everything is up to date. At the end of the year you should look to produce an income and expenditure sheet for presentation to the rest of the group, so that people can be satisfied that their money has been put to good use. If you can get this audited by an independent but friendly accountant, it will show potential funders that you are a responsible and well-organised group.

Taxes, rates and PAYE

Most small local groups are unlikely to have to pay taxes of any kind. However you may need to register for VAT if you are bringing in and spending more than £58,000 a year (2004/05 figure). If you think this may affect you, get advice from your local CVS and then contact your local Customs and Excise office. They are there to help you and give free advice.

If you occupy a building or land you may be liable to pay business rates to your local authority. Registered charities receive a 50% discount by law and many authorities use their discretion to reduce rates to charities to a minimum level. In any event it is always worth asking for a reduction.

If you directly employ staff you will have to register with the Inland Revenue for the operation of PAYE. In some areas an organisation such as CVS may be able to undertake payroll operations for small groups at a reasonable charge. In some cases funders will also pay money to a larger 'accountable body' who can keep records and provide accounts and payments for a smaller community group.

Becoming a charity

Some groups put a lot of effort into registering as a charity. This can have many advantages, in terms of fundraising: some bodies will only make grants to charities. But it does involve a lot more bureaucracy and record-keeping. Setting up as a trust (see Part 2.6) may be a lot easier in the first instance. Get advice on this before taking any action.

How much money do we need?

If you have a clear plan for what the group should do, then it should also be pretty clear where you need to spend money. If you don't have such a plan, turn to Part 2.5 and develop one!

You should aim to have a clear idea of what money be needed for and when it will be needed – ideally for the whole year ahead. You will certainly need this if you are to raise external funds.

There are basically two types of costs: capital (or project) costs and revenue (or ongoing) costs. The project costs are what you need to develop and carry through your proposed project, while the ongoing costs are what it costs to run your organisation. These latter costs may be low or non-existent if you are a group set up simply to run a one-off project, but if your group is going to last longer than that, then the revenue costs will be important. This is important because funders are often happy to fund projects and less keen to simply fund ongoing group work. Many groups have found themselves with money to do interesting things but unable to pay the rent on their office: this is not ideal!

The key is to link your project to your revenue as closely as possible. This is something that new groups may neglect. If, for instance, your office in the community centre is being used for even a small part of the project and is the base for the administration of the project then the project should certainly pay some or most of the rent and other associated costs. Don't leave these kinds of things out of project budgets. You should also have a very clear idea of how much it costs to run the organisation for a year in terms of office costs, newsletters and postage, website costs, transport etc. These are the costs that underpin all your work.

Raising money

Most groups can raise some money fairly easily. Fifty people paying a membership fee of £4 each may cover basic costs of distributing a newsletter. A 'whip-round' at the end of a good meeting may do more than cover the costs of the meeting, and a jumble sale can raise much needed start-up costs. But if you are going to do any major work you need to look beyond your members and your community.

There are several sources of grants for small projects. BTCV produces a printed 'Grants and Awards Fact Sheet' which is also available on the website (www.btcv.org) and that is the first place to start looking. The GreenSpaces publication (available from www.btcv.org/shop) also has useful information. Your local Voluntary Action Bureau, or Community Council, should know about local grant funds, and produce newsletters with regular updates on national funding streams like the Big Lottery Fund. Some local radio and TV stations and local authorities also run their own schemes.

Raising money is a skill – some would say an art – and some people are very good at it. If you like doing it then stick with it; if you don't then find some people who do and encourage them to get training to do it well. Bear in mind that all funders have limits: you are often in competition with other groups, and also with groups supported by professional fundraisers.

SUCCESS IN FUNDRAISING

The National Lotteries Charities Board has cited the following reasons for bids being unsuccessful: one in four bids fail due to inadequate planning or proposals for managing the project; one in seven bids fail because they are for projects that do not contribute to the Board's aims; one in 10 bids are turned down due to a lack of funds.

Don't be surprised if you get rejected, especially at first. Instead find people with experience who are prepared to help your group. Some groups who have paid fundraisers to help them say that this is an excellent way forward (and they're the ones for whom the fundraisers were successful!), but this needs careful thought and planning. Don't use a fundraiser without finding out what they have really done: get references from groups they have helped.

CASE STUDY: BUSY LIZZIES IN SHADWELL

The Busy Lizzies are a group of Bengali women who live in East London's Shadwell. For several years they have worked to improve the run-down areas of their community, turning them into restful green spaces bursting with plants. They were then awarded a BTCV People's Places Award of £8000. With this they were able to formalise their group and expand the project, involving more members of the local community. They held community planting days where they invited members of the local community to join them. The mornings were spent planting shrubs and plants and also planting up hanging baskets which they were then able to take away.

You can raise money in many ways:
- Apply for a Local Authority, lottery or charitable trust grant;
- Get a local company to make a donation or gift-in-kind (materials, expertise etc); and
- Hold fundraising events.

What you do will depend partly on the amount of money that you need and when you will need it. You may need to put together a funding package – getting money from a number of different sources, possibly using some or all of the above methods. This will relate in part to our budget and your project plan.

You also need to be aware that getting funding is rarely done quickly. While some local grant sources (such as small regeneration project funds) can offer a decision rapidly, it usually takes three or four months before you hear one way or the other. This needs to be planned in to your work.

There are no easy or guaranteed ways to make money but there are some pointers to success:
- Funders like to see that groups applying for money are able to raise a certain amount of the money they require on their own. This match funding can often include volunteer time and gifts-in-kind.
- Be absolutely clear about how much you need and what it will be spent on. The more accurate and realistic your costings and design plans, the more seriously your application will be taken.
- Make sure that your proposal fits the criteria that the funder is looking for. You may need to highlight a particular aspect of your project to take account of the funders' priorities.
- Make sure that you're using the current year's application form, as sometimes they vary from year to year, as can funders' priorities. A phone call is usually enough to confirm this.
- Make sure your accounts are up-to-date and preferably audited.
- Give yourself sufficient time to devote to fundraising, taking note of when you want to start work, the deadlines for applications, and the dates when grants are awarded.
- Convey the environmental and the wider community benefits of your proposed work: how will it improve people's health, or break down barriers between communities or create jobs. Think this through and put it in the application.

The Getting Results programme operates in Birmingham and in parts of the Black Country. BTCV and The Refugee Council in the West Midlands are aiming to help to break down the distrust and misunderstandings which cause so much misplaced controversy around the asylum seeking process and to create opportunities for asylum seekers to participate in community environmental projects to combat feelings of social isolation and prejudice. Young asylum seekers are at a particular social disadvantage due to cultural and linguistic barriers and prohibition on mainstream education, training or employment. It can take up to between six months and four years for asylum cases to be concluded and there is a desperate need for those housed in temporary accommodation to receive ongoing support.

Funding from the Commission for Racial Equality's Getting Results programme has allowed asylum seekers in the West Midlands area to get involved in voluntary work to improve the local community. The Getting Results project aims to:

- Enable at least 50 asylum seekers living in the West Midlands to make a positive contribution to the local environment;
- Enable asylum seekers to integrate with mainstream volunteering activities and local communities;
- Enable asylum seekers to increase their knowledge of their local area and to increase their sense of belonging within the local community;
- Enable asylum seekers to use the local environment to relieve some of the stresses and tensions of daily life that they experience; and
- Enable the local community to see the positive contribution that asylum seekers can make to the local environment.

The project has been developed by BTCV and the Refugee Council West Midlands. Through a variety of practical conservation activities, participants are able to gain local knowledge and forge links with local people. The benefits extend far beyond pure practical conservation skills. In a neutral outdoor environment away from the pressure of their temporary housing, individuals can benefit from urban green spaces, mix freely, improve their English language skills and gain satisfaction from making a difference to the local environment.

The programme organises a range of events and activities including: practical conservation work; growing vegetables at an local allotment; Green Gym work, which offers an outdoor environment for people to get fit and engage in conservation; and walks and trips to nature reserves.

Some recent Getting Results work includes:
- Green Gym Project, Sandwell

Focusing on the health benefits of conservation work, these activities begin and end with stretching exercises, run for just two to three hours and are a great way of getting fit.

- Taster days

This series of 'taster days' enable asylum seekers to visit the various projects and decide which may be most appropriate for themselves. A recent 'taster day' involved a group of asylum seekers from countries including Togo, Congo, Ethiopia, Guinea and the Yemen. As soon as they were dropped off from the minibus into a neutral, outdoor environment, the benefits of this project became clear. People were able to mix freely, enjoy the sunshine and relax away from the pressures of their temporary housing.

The day began with a visit to the Green Gym site in Sandwell where work was being done to plant native bulbs and plants close to a public footpath. All participants were keen to learn and do something practical with their hands: one talked (in French) about how he had worked on his father's farm in Togo. This is a group who on average have been housed in temporary accommodation on average for four months, who have little chance to enjoy green space or interact with members of the community outside of their accommodation.

The group also did translated words into siimple English, learning the names of birds and animals ,and general conversation work. For many, this was the first time they had been out on a project: 'I don't get a chance usually to learn English and chat to people outside. I've learned so many new words today'.

The results suggest that volunteering has many positive influences on asylum seeker groups as well as the local community, irrespective of a community's social class or wealth. Specific benefits to date include:
- Enabling asylum seekers to make a positive contribution to the local environment;
- Allowing opportunities for asylum seekers to positively integrate with mainstream volunteering activities and local communities;
- Giving asylum seekers an improved knowledge/ familiarity of local area, leading to increased sense of belonging/security/confidence and, therefore, increasing their ability to lead a more active life within the local area and reduce alienation;
- Enabling asylum seekers to be able to use the local environment to relieve stress, tension and improve their quality of life;
- Creating opportunities for the promotion of the positive contributions that asylum seekers will have made to the local environment; and
- Creating opportunities for learning English.

The programme helps to improve the public perception of asylum seekers, and helps break down the distrust and misunderstandings which cause so much prejudice. BTCV is looking to continue and develop this work in co-operation with Refugee Action and the Refugee Council as well as local Asylum Support Teams and Social Services staff.

- Be realistic: don't make claims that you can never live up to. If someone comes to assess your proposal, they will probably spot the exaggerations and will reject your application as a result.
- Have a carefully prepared bid that is properly thought through, well presented and checked for accuracy. It will give confidence in your ability to carry out the project. Keep copies of your completed application for reference purposes.

- Send in your application in good time for the closing date.

Finally, be creative! Make your project sound interesting, exciting, and open to as many people as possible. Think about the person doing the assessment: they may have read 300 applications before they get to yours. The one that stands out by having exciting and unusual ideas that look like they will really work is most likely to catch the decision-maker's eye.

Part 2.8
Is it making a difference?

Monitoring or evaluation – what's the difference?

It is easy to see if community projects have been effective by just looking at what they set out to do and whether they achieved it. If a project said they'd plant a hundred trees in a neighbourhood and they did so then it's easy to say 'job done!' and tick the box. That's the **monitoring** approach.

But there's a lot that such an approach doesn't tell us:

- Who planted the trees – was it a hundred local people, two hundred local school children or five overworked professional tree planters?
- Are they in the places where local people said they'd like trees or are they in lines round the edge of the park?
- How many of the trees were dug up to plant in people's gardens?
- How many were vandalised in the first six months?
- Do local people think the area looks better for having the trees?

Answering these sorts of questions is where **evaluation** comes in (see below).

Projects need to be monitored. Not only is it important that we know that we've done what we said we'd do, but the funders will also expect a report at the end of the project to say that the targets and outputs were met (or to explain why they were not). Evaluation is also important: we need to find out if the outcomes of the projects – the aims we were hoping to achieve – have happened.

Monitoring and evaluation are often only carried out at the end of a project (probably to report to the funders). But if you wait until then, it's too late to change anything. You need to start while there is still time to learn from the successes and mistakes.

If you want your work to flourish and be successful, then it is important to make monitoring and evaluation part of your project right from the start. This can help you to:

- Run the project better;
- Spot little problems before they become big problems; and
- Make your next project even more successful.

Making it work

Monitoring matters. It's important and simple to carry out: set out a series of measurable goals and take regular measurements to see whether you've reached those goals.

If your project is a quick one (such as in the tree planting example), then the monitoring is indeed easily carried out at the end. But most projects last quite a bit longer, and for that reason you'll need to start by setting not just final targets but interim ones too. Ask what you will need to do in the first three and six months, as well as two years down the road. This is an important part of project planning (see Part 2.5). Then make sure you set up a three and six month review to see if those targets have been achieved. If not then you need to ask why, and to make some changes so that the next targets don't go astray as well.

The Healthy Walks project in Scotland aims to open up the great outdoors and beauty of the Scottish countryside to everyone. The project is aimed at people living in the heart of urban Glasgow, who would not normally have the opportunity to experience the Highlands and Islands, and provides a fantastic opportunity to break out of the city into the fresh air. A diverse range of community groups are involved from wide-ranging backgrounds, such as China, Zimbabwe, Russia, Bangladesh, as well as the local Scots. For many, the outdoors can be an alien place. Most have little idea of where to go walking and how to travel there without their own transport. This EfA project is inclusive to all and reflects the rich diversity of Glasgow's multi-cultural communities, including local residents, disadvantaged social groups, asylum seekers and refugees. It has identified a real need in the city to provide a service to ensure 'everyone' has access to the countryside. For example, many of the women involved are unable to leave the urban environment due to child-care constraints or are uneasy leaving the city alone. This project is an innovative way to engage community groups and promote feelings of well-being by opening up access to quality green space.

The Healthy Walks always featured in the EfA project in Scotland and in May 2004 the walks developed further with a 'herbal discovery' walk around the shores of picturesque Loch Katrine. The group then began to work together to raise their fitness levels. The volunteers for the day were also joined by BBC Radio 4's walking show, *Ramblings*.

The programme has progressed a step further into a 'hill-walking' club, tackling Scottish munros. The combined efforts to keep fit, as well as interest in the environment has overcome many problems, including integration and language barriers.

A programme of four hill walks were organised in the Strathblane hills and around Scotland's highest village, Wanlockhead. The hills were used as an 'outdoor classroom' to raise awareness of biodiversity in Scotland. The group are especially proud of their outstanding achievement when 19 people reached the summit of Ben Lomond accompanied by two mountain leaders and Polly Murray – the first and youngest British woman to climb Mount Everest.

The programme to date has been an unbridled success, introducing many socially excluded groups from a multitude of nationalities to the outdoors and Scottish hills. This project has blown away two myths; one that disadvantaged or ethnic groups are not interested in the environment, and secondly that people from such groups do not volunteer.

It is quite common not to meet targets. It can take longer than expected to get things moving, for instance one or two key people can't make a meeting so a decision is put off for a month; a staff person leaves and it takes two or three months to get a replacement; the people supplying the key materials deliver the goods late; or, perhaps it pours with rain on the day of the big community action.

All these things can happen. The key to success is not to ignore them. Look for other ways of doing things, manage the risk of delay, change your project plan accordingly and be aware of things that may cause not just delays but also major problems. Most funders are happy to accept changes to projects and continue funding them if they know what's gone wrong and why.

Evaluating awareness

Many projects talk about raising awareness, but very few can tell you what level that awareness is before they start (or even how you should measure it). This highlights the need for a 'base-line' survey – a survey of how things currently stand before you commence the project, which can then be compared against later surveys to check progress and awareness of your work. If you carry out a survey right at the start (for example, of what people think about the area), you will have some real data to base your final evaluation on. This may be time-consuming at the start, but it can produce very valuable results.

Beyond monitoring

Good monitoring systems are important for good evaluation, but evaluation is about a lot more than just measuring. Evaluation can help us to be clear on:
- What has been done;
- What has happened as a result;
- How far the objectives have been met;
- What the group and the community have learned;
- What to do next; and
- How to do things better next time.

Evaluation is all part of the learning process. People need to learn about what has worked and what has not. It is also central to community empowerment – people need to see how they are making a difference. Developing a good evaluation process takes time and care, especially if we are to assess issues such as involvement and participation. There will be a need for both quantitative (how much have we done?) and qualitative (how well did we do it?) assessment.

It is also important to evaluate so that you know what local people think about the project, and how the work your group has done has helped meet their needs. To do this, you need to involve the community in the evaluation right from the start.

Developing an evaluation programme

The key to success in evaluation is to see what's actually happening and to evaluate every aspect. If you take a long look at any project you will see that there are four broad areas that you can evaluate and it's good to look at them all.

These four parts of the 'project cycle' are:

- Inputs: these are the resources that go in to a project. These are material resources (money, the use of buildings, equipment etc); human resources (people's time) and the resources put in by support agencies. Those people include local people but may also include outside advisors and local council staff. A very simple measure here would be the number of volunteers involved in a project, and the hours or days of work that they put in.

- Processes: the ways in which the inputs are used to lead towards desired outputs and outcomes. Look through your project plan and you will see that all sorts of things happen as part of the project: these are the processes and each one can go well or not so well. This all depends partly how people work together, how they take decisions, and how they gain knowledge. This is not something that people often measure, but if the process goes wrong, you usually know pretty fast, since people stop helping or getting involved!

- Outputs: these are the specific products of a project. These are the things which the project intends to deliver: for example, the number of people who get involved, the number of trees planted and the number of leaflets. The outputs are not usually the aims of the project: they are the means by which the aims can be achieved. The outputs are usually fairly easy to measure and are a key part of any monitoring process.

- Outcomes: these are the effects which we hope the outputs and the processes will produce. These will relate to the very first questions you asked at the start of the project planning process. If you achieve these then you have met the original goals of the project. These indirect results may not be so directly measurable, but it is usually quite easy to develop some questions to help this work. Bear in mind that outcomes may not be in direct control of your organisation because they will also depend on the actions of others.

If an output is, for instance, a youth club attended by 30 young people two nights a week for one year, then the outcomes could include less youth crime, more co-operation between different groups of young people, increased confidence in the young people, and perhaps more young people getting jobs. You have to be careful as to how far your outcomes are related just to your project, but often one project is part of a longer-term programme of community development.

ACTION POINT

**Evaluate a tree! Ask yourself and your group:
What are the outputs and outcomes of a tree?
What are the inputs and processes?
Put together your responses and discuss them
with your group. This can be a good way of getting
people thinking about evaluation. The outputs may
be easy to assess (they may include timber,
flowers and fruit, for example), but how many
long-term outcomes are there?**

Good evaluation is important not just to show what's been done, but also to look at what the group has learned and to show how members feel about what has been done. That's why it's important to consider all these issues. Here is an example of an evaluation for a project:

INPUTS
- Staff time and skills
- Partner staff time and skills
- Skills of local community
- Funds and support from funding partners
- Political and strategic contexts
- Work completed by contractors
- Work completed by artists
- Training delivered by external trainers
- Other community activity
- Contacts
- Land (derelict or otherwise) and agreement to use it

PROCESS
- Community group meetings to plan the process
- Awareness raising
- Other consultation processes
- Programme/project development
- Design work with community
- Training needs assessment
- Training
- Team-building
- Networking
- Physical project building
- Celebration
- Support for local groups
- Monitoring and Evaluation

OUTPUTS
- Attendance at regular group meetings
- Constituted group set up
- Numbers of people actively involved
- Facility provided
- Qualifications and training for numbers of people
- Partnership group set up
- Number of volunteers developed
- Number of people volunteering
- Area of land improved

OUTCOMES
- Empowered community
- People gaining new skills and confidence from training and project work
- More secure environment
- More useable environment
- Increased awareness
- Bigger ambitions
- Spin-off projects
- More confidence amongst people
- Increased community pride and identity
- Closer partner relations
- World saved!

If you have been involved in any similar projects, you may be able to think of other outputs and outcomes from such a project. The difficult aspect is to be found in judging what the outcomes are from the project in comparison to changes, which have naturally have occurred in the area.

You can develop indicators to measure both the outputs and outcomes from any project and measure these regularly. More information on evaluation can be found on the website of the Community Development Foundation (www.cdf.org.uk). This process is listed there as 'ABCD – Achieving Better Community Development' and there are full details about materials and training courses.

Evaluating involvement and participation

It can seem as if participation and involvement are some of the hardest things to evaluate, not least because every case is different. However it is possible to assess and evaluate what you have done using some basic measures. These include assessing:

- The percentage of questionnaires returned in target areas;
- The number of people attending meetings;
- The number of people (and age range, diversity etc) in community steering groups;
- The number of residents coming into the group;
- The number of events organised by the community;
- The number of door-to-door surveys;
- The number of local people in formal positions

(eg running the surveys);
- The number of local people with decision-making power in the project; and
- The number of people from different minority ethnic groups participating (in respect to the make-up of the overall population in the area).

What these will not always tell you is how successful you have been. If 20 people turn up at a meeting then this would count as excellent if you are located in a small village, but not so good if you are involved in a city-wide planning exercise. The 'bottom line' can often be derived by asking the people you have worked with and involved: what did they think? Has it been useful for them? What did they learn? What did they think about the project? These may be difficult questions, but they provide some of the most valuable answers because they will tell those running the project how they personally have worked with the others involved.

The bottom line on evaluation is two-fold:
- It can help you understand and learn from failure This is the best way of making sure it doesn't happen again, so don't be afraid to acknowledge and analyse it.
- It can help show that progress is being made. Many communities often express the idea that 'nothing is changing, and if it is, it's getting worse'. This can make it hard to involve people. A good evaluation, done with the local community, can show that the efforts that you and they have made together really are making a difference.

Patchway is a densely populated area in Bristol with a wide range of poverty and health problems. An area of land near to the Prudential-owned Mall at Cribbs Causeway is the only significant green space for miles around and is also home to a 400-year-old woodland and to nationally scarce species of plants and animals.

Local community group, Patchway Conservation Group approached BTCV for help improve the site. This is an already well-established group of local volunteers who are working with English Nature and other key agencies to establish their own programme of conservation activity in and around the Patchway area. BTCV and the Grass Roots programme donated £10,000 to the project to help drive regeneration for people and wildlife in communities near to Prudential-owned properties. The local authority had also identified a number of other public green spaces in Patchway that had low key community involvement and which could form a potential wildlife corridor of high biodiversity value and to help link up communities and schools.

The sites were heavily-used public rights of way, but neglected green spaces. Many of the trees were vandalised, the footpaths were difficult to use and the area covered in litter – a poor resource for people and wildlife.

In partnership with local community groups, BTCV and the Grass Roots programme worked to help regenerate the land and to provide a rich urban oasis for all in the community. The aim was to involve the local community in improving the sites, to reduce vandalism, provide educational value, and encourage biodiversity, while providing the local community with a valuable site for exercise and leisure.

The project has included developing a sustainable management plan that has helped to balance the needs of all concerned through activities such as:

- Footpath improvement, hedging, dry stone walling and rubbish clearance;
- Training in practical conservation for local schools and adults;
- The creation of a new pond;
- Habitat management: scrub clearance, coppicing, tree planting, tree seed collection and planting, and planting hedgerows; and
- A series of guided walks to encourage adults and children to learn about the local area.

BTCV involved local schools in the educational and practical aspects of conservation, working with them to produce a walks leaflet, schools nature pack and website.

BTCV uses the environment to connect with young people, offering them opportunities to contribute to the decision making process. We have found that involving young people in worthwhile environmental projects helps them take ownership of the area. A major public consultation event was organised for this project, specifically targeting young people to ensure their voices were heard. It was attended by over 150 people, including local schoolchildren who discussed ideas about what to do with the green space. What emerged was that there was a lack of recreational facilities and as a result there has been a commitment from the local authority to create a bike track.

The achievements have been substantial:

- Over 500 local people were involved in the project, including schoolchildren, residents, staff from The Mall at Cribbs Causeway, and the conservation group;
- 100 people attended the public event to celebrate the site being designated as a local nature reserve;

- Many young people who were previously excluded from the site can now access it;
- Activities such as dry stone walling, pond dipping, conservation management, skills in flora and fauna were carried out. Bird boxes were installed;
- The project involved 80 volunteer workdays worth over £4,000; and
- 10 practical workday events were organised.

The direct environmental benefits include the conservation of an ancient woodland which has helped to preserve and increase the biodiversity of the site.

The longer-term outcomes are many and varied:

- Reduction in damage and vandalism to the site;
- The increased awareness of the area also encouraged more local people to benefit from this public space;
- Greater confidence among local people;
- Development of a sense of ownership and pride in the local environment;
- Local volunteers and schools played a vital role in the maintenance of the park; and
- As well as access to green space, residents now have a safer and more accessible walking route to the local shops, which has also encouraged a reduction in the use of cars.

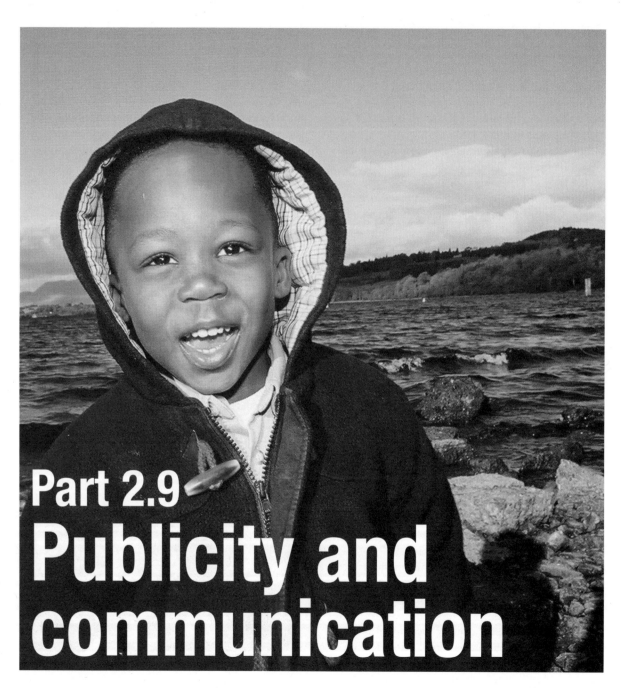

Part 2.9
Publicity and communication

Whatever kind of work you are planning you need to communicate with people. For some small projects you may only need to talk with the people involved, but in most cases there'll be all sorts of people who'll want to know what you are planning (and who will probably want to add their ideas and opinions). On top of that, most voluntary programmes want to attract and involve people: if you're going to do that then people need to hear about you.

Communicating well

Communication is important in everything you do, whether it's talking one-to-one with someone or appearing on TV or producing a newsletter. Experts will tell you that communication is:

- At least 55% behaviour – the way we act, the way we pay attention to people, our body language and the clothes we wear all send messages to people.
- About 38% is the way we speak (not what we say) – the tone of voice and the volume: speaking loudly or quietly will send very different messages (think about this next time you're on the phone to someone). It may also be about the way we write – contrast a hand-written letter with a hurried e-mail.
- Only about 7% of communication is about the words we use.

In short – you are communicating all the time so it makes sense to try and do it well.

Communication is also a two-way process – it's as much about listening as it is about talking. How many times have you felt frustrated because someone hasn't been listening when you've been trying to tell them something you think is important? For anyone running a project, being a good communicator is vital.

Communication is very important at key points in a project – for instance, the way you welcome and involve a new volunteer in the first few minutes makes all the difference about how far they become involved.

Towards better practice

Think of three or four important communication challenges in the life of your project, such as talking with a potential funder. For each one, think about (and perhaps write down) the key issues that you want to communicate (and who you would communicate to) and consider how you can get your point across as well as possible.

Being aware of how you communicate is a continuous process, and discussion with other people you are working with about this may help. It is worth putting some time aside (once you've got to know each other well) for a session on communication. It could be a chance for you to advise each other on how you are perceived (in an open and friendly manner!!) and to determine how the whole project is communicated to other people.

Effective publicity

Publicity is about how your work is perceived by others, and that is central to your success. You need to have good publicity in order to:

- Tell people what you do (and why they should care about it);
- Get people and organisations involved;
- Recruit volunteers; and
- Show your funders and partners that you are doing good work

Publicity is a lot more than simply a leaflet or a poster, and like many aspects of your work, it is more effective if you have a plan or strategy. It also involves a wide range of skills: ask around the group to find if there are people already involved who have skills such as:

- Art and design (for those posters, leaflets and newsletters);
- Using computer design packages;
- Writing (for leaflets and press releases etc); and
- Public speaking.

If you can't find anyone who's done this work before, then it's worth looking around for some support from other organisations. In reality, however, it's not that difficult to make publicity work, as long as you plan it well and put time and effort in. Your publicity should always aim to:

- Let people know you exist;
- Show people that taking part in your activities is easy, fun, safe, satisfying and benefits their environment; and
- Encourage them to get involved and give them the information they need to do so.

CASE STUDY: WEST INDIAN ASSOCIATION GARDEN, OLDHAM

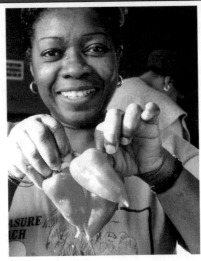

BTCV is working with the West Indian Association in Oldham to develop a community garden in an outdoor area that is currently run-down, under used and neglected. The garden has become run down and vandalised. There is also a big litter problem.

The project involves women from an over 50s Afro-Caribbean ladies' group. They are taking part in gardening workshops aimed at giving them horticultural skills and knowledge, and other associated skills. Aspects of healthy living are also being introduced with food growing sessions and the exercise benefits of being outdoors and gardening.

Children from the Poinciana Education Project have been involved in the design and development of the garden. The end results are both a vibrant community resource and a group of local people who have developed the necessary skills and expertise to ensure the garden's ongoing care and maintenance.

There are many guides to effective publicity and the BTCV Local Action handbook (available at www.btcv.org) has more advice, but these points should help you get started.

Developing a publicity strategy

If you've got something you want to publicise (it doesn't matter whether it's a new project, a book or simply a jumble sale) then decide:

● Who you are trying to reach;
● Exactly what do you want them to know?; and
● What do you want them to do?

If it's a jumble sale it's pretty clear: you want to tell people who live near the venue that it's on Saturday 4 October at 2pm, and that you want them to come and buy things! However, it's not always that simple.

Your publicity strategy should also relate to your overall objectives. If you have a target of involving 200 young people in a project over two months, then your publicity will be quite different to that of a project looking to get 20 people along for an afternoon.

Be clear about your objectives for promotion and publicity. These are the things you are looking to achieve, and they should be realistic, achievable, relevant and timely. They must also be clearly understandable by everyone.

An example objective for a community centre might be: 'we want to have the centre used as much as possible by people organising activities that local people can take parting and enjoy'. The publicity objective could then be: 'to promote the centre so that as many local people as possible know what is going on here and feel confident and happy to come and take part in the activities that interest them.' Once you've set this out, then it should be clearer how you will plan your publicity.

Your plan needs to address the following:
● What resources do we have in terms of people, time, skills, equipment, money? This is important: don't try something wildly ambitious that then fails to deliver.
● Is this the right time to be doing this kind of publicity and do we have enough time to plan it? You should start planning a good few weeks before any specific event.
● How will we know if it has worked? It's always good to have some success criteria: if only five people turn up for the jumble sale and buy just one thing each you will need to do better next time.

Define your audiences

There will undoubtedly be many 'audiences'. Each community within the locality where you are working is likely to respond best to different types of publicity. For example, text messages may work badly with people over 60; similarly, a piece in the parish newsletter probably wouldn't bring in that many young people. Getting people's mobile phone numbers is a very useful way of building a rapid communication network.

Work out with people in the group exactly who you are aiming to communicate with. It may be all the stakeholders you identified in Part 2.2, or it may be a few groups within that wider list. It all depends what you want to achieve!

Be clear about your messages

There may also be different messages that work better with different audiences. Try and be as clear as possible about what you are trying to tell people. And keep it simple. If you want people to get involved in work on a site, make it sound interesting and fun – don't deluge people with information about the valuable biodiversity of the site which their work will help improve. You can tell them more once they've got involved. You may also want to use different ways to reinforce a message to one group (see 'choosing your media' in the next column).

ACTION POINT
Towards better practice
Think about what makes you decide to go and see a particular film. You may read a review in a paper (and another in a magazine), you see the trailer in the cinema (and the poster on a hoarding), and you might check the film times on the internet. Or someone may simply tell you it's really good.

Now think about and list (in the same way) what different ways people will hear about what you are doing: are there gaps in your strategy?

Choosing your media

There are a great many 'media' these days, and choosing the right mix is important. Some are almost free; others are expensive, and may be inappropriate in any case.

A good starting point is to look for the ones that are free or low cost. A good press release may get your news into five local papers for the cost of some paper and a stamp (or even just an e-mail). Many local organisations will have paper or electronic newsletters: find out who has these, when they go out, who they go out to, and find out how you can get your information in. Some people will be happy for you to write an article; others will want to take your information and fit it in to their own style.

A basic printed leaflet or 'flyer' on coloured paper is often a good starting point for any local event: it's easy to produce and photocopy and can be stuck through letter boxes and in shop windows or sent out with mailings. Again keep it simple: make sure it says: 'who, what, where and when'.

However, you may want to step it up a little: you might want a logo for your group or a photo; you may want to go for colour printing and you may want a smart poster to highlight an important event. This is where skills and perhaps professional experience come in: if you are not confident about designing and have never completed a design role before, get some help. Your local CVS may be able to help or advise. If there's a local group who has excellent publicity ask them how they do it; you could also look for any local person who works as a designer and see if they're prepared to help in their local community.

Don't get too carried away: remember to keep within your resources and focused on who you are aiming at. And don't forget that the best medium is often word of mouth. In a small community this can be fast and free, but do be aware of who may be excluded.

Working with journalists and the press

The standard way to get the press interested in your work is to send out a good press release. Guidance on how to do this is in the BTCV Local Action handbook. But you should also seek to develop a good relationship with your local papers (and radio stations). Read the paper regularly: note the names of journalists who write the stories that cover your kinds of activities. Send them a press release as well as sending one to the main news desk and ring them and tell them more. Invite them to cover the event. The more you can develop a relationship with them, the more likely you are to get good coverage in the newspaper and on local radio.

At the same time, it's important not to deluge them with material. If you send them too much information about routine events they will switch off: plan your approaches to the press as part of your publicity strategy. If you talk with them, they'll tell you what is interesting and what is not.

Press work should also reflect your context. If you're working in a very deprived area it may be one that generates lots of negative stories about crime, drugs and vandalism. Avoid doing anything that can help build such stereotypes and try to ensure that they start to feature positive stores about the area.

Diverse audiences

Marketing professionals will tell you that the key to success is 'segmentation' – splitting people into different groups and targeting those groups in ways that appeal to them. It's just the same with publicity. As above, text messaging works well with young people (assuming you can get the numbers to text); other communities need other approaches. Identify all the media such as magazines and newsletters that go to different ethnic groups, and don't forget the simple local ones: a notice read out by a parish priest (or in a mosque or synagogue) may target exactly the people you want for a specific event better than anything else.

PHOTOGRAPHY AND VIDEO RECORDING
Photographs and film or video are an essential part of publicity, and digital cameras are making it easier to produce your own. All newspaper reporters will expect to be able to take photographs, or ask you to submit them for inclusion in the paper. You may also want to take photographs to use in displays and reports to funders. While most adults are happy about having their photograph taken it is important to be aware of some restrictions.

All children under 16 years of age should not be photographed without permission from a parent or adult who is responsible for them. This is now accepted good practice by schools, sports, youth organisations and local councils. It is also the case that many Muslim people do not want their photographs to be taken on the grounds that displaying the human image is sacrilegious.

If you are having photographs taken or activities are being filmed you should make this clear to people. 'Consent slips' should be available for signature at any community event. For children this must be signed by a parent/carer or guardian. Bear in mind that you do not generally have the right to pass on information about any individual without their prior permission.

As with design, there are some things that are better done by skilled people. If you're planning to use photographs for brochures or permanent displays don't rely on a friend who has a camera – you may not get the results you want. Suggest that as many group members as possible take shots, and see if a local newspaper will send a photographer along. If you want to be confident of the results, and you can afford it, see how much a local professional costs. Get them to come early and spend time with them discussing the story that you want to illustrate. They may well spot other aspects, so consider their ideas. Get them to take plenty of pictures and work with them to select the ones that fit your purpose.

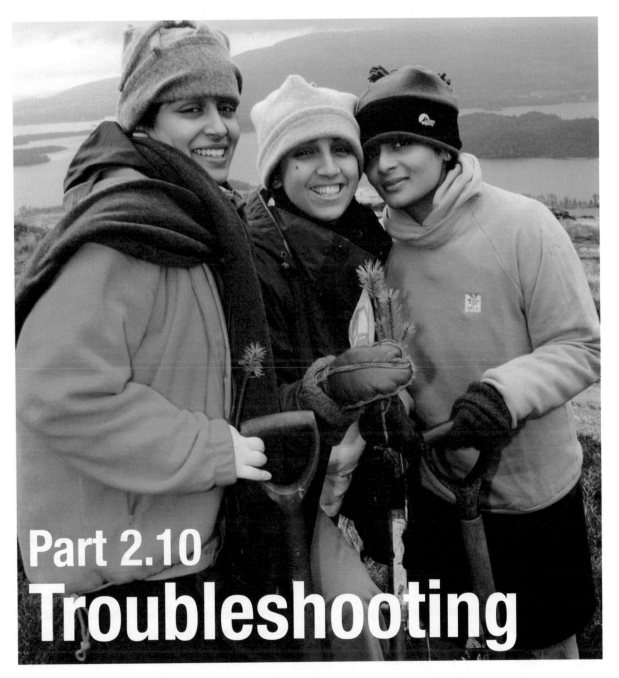

Part 2.10
Troubleshooting

Whatever the project you are running there will doubtless be problems. Some are easy to deal with; others a lot harder, but quite a few can be dealt with before they start by good planning, and managing the risks. Bigger problems can arise even if you think you have identified all the risks, so you do need to be aware of what to do and how to avoid them.

This section looks at:
● Working out what problems may arise;
● Health and safety issues; and
● Personal safety.

What's your problem? – assessing the risks

As they say on TV: 'what could possibly go wrong?', and that's the basis for 'risk assessment'. It is what it says it is: an exercise to help you assess all the likely risks that are associated with your project. As such this should be the starting point for all your work and you should be especially aware of potential risks as you plan your project (see Part 2.5).

Risk assessment is about hazards and risks. The hazards are the things that could go wrong and cause harm, illness or injury or damage to property; the risk is the likelihood of that harm actually taking place.

Assessing risk is a three-stage process:
● Identifying the hazards;
● Assessing the level of risk associated with the hazards; and
● Taking steps to cut the risks.

This may sound complicated but we all assess risks all the time: crossing a road involves checking the traffic and assessing whether we can get across before the next car comes (and what happens if we slip and so on).

Assessing the risks for your project involves a set of questions:
● How likely is it that something will go wrong?
● If it did go wrong how serious would the result be?
● How often does the risk arise? (eg daily, every time a particular tool is used, once a year etc)
● How many people would be affected?
● Are the effects immediate or will they only appear a long time after the event (chronic)?
● What does the law dictate? Are there any specific regulations covering this hazard?

To make life easier there is a range of standard risk assessment forms. Your local BTCV office can help with this, and there are very useful short courses on BTCV Training (www.btcv.org/training). If you want to go into more detail on this, perhaps for a large project, BTCV has produced a learning resource pack which is available from BTCV Enterprises on 01302 572200.

You should seek to assess the overall level of risk as 'high', 'medium' or 'low'. If a project is 'high' risk you should immediately consider whether to proceed! The important thing is, of course, not just to assess the risks, but to take action to cut these risks to a minimum. Think especially about those risks that are both fairly likely and will have very serious consequences if things do go wrong. Think carefully about the risks to vulnerable groups, such as children, the elderly, people with disabilities or pregnant or nursing women.

If there are risks don't ignore them and hope they'll go away. Talk the issues through with someone you trust – your manager, if you have one, or with other organisations who may have experience of similar situations.

Health and safety issues

Plenty of projects will have very low risks and few safety problems. But if you are doing any outdoor work involving tools – and that includes spades as much as chainsaws – then there are health and safety issues. You need to tackle these, not least because if something does go wrong, you and any local organisation may be legally liable.

The key to safety is making sure that people are properly looked after. That entails 'PPE' or 'personal protective equipment'. This may include:
- Protective gloves;
- Goggles;
- Safety helmets;
- Safety footwear; and
- Reflective waistcoats.

Get advice from BTCV, your local parks department or any other experienced source about what you will need if you are planning practical conservation work. They may well be able to lend you some or all of the necessary equipment.

Be aware of the specific needs and circumstances of the people you are working with. People with learning difficulties and those who speak little or no English may not understand safety instructions or emergency warnings. If you are leading such work then you are responsible for ensuring that safety guidance has been understood. More information is available in various BTCV publications (these can be downloaded from the website (www.btcv.org), but if you are planning on leading long-term work you should get some training.

Working with children and young people

Work with children raises some very specific problems. If you are working with young people you should have at least some training with regard to these issues, and you will need to have a criminal records check (unless you're based in Northern Ireland. If so, check for procedure with NI Volunteer Development Agency on 028 9023 6100 or www.volunteering_ni.org). Obviously if you are running a local project and young people turn up to take part in voluntary work, you will not wish to turn them away but you should not be in a supervisory position if you are not trained.

There is a Home Office publication *Safe from Harm – a Code of Practice for Safeguarding the Welfare of Children in Voluntary Organisations in England and Wales*, which gives suggestions on ways to minimise opportunities for abuse of young people. There are similar publications for Scotland and Northern Ireland.

CASE STUDY: CONSERVATION AND CONFIDENCE

Young people aged between 16 and 19 years of age considered at risk of social exclusion have been engaged on a programme of practical conservation work, team-building activities and social events. Some of the young people on this programme were homeless and others had been through intensive drug rehabilitation, so these activities represented a significant challenge for many of the people involved.

The project served the regions of Milton Keynes, Oxfordshire and Buckinghamshire. The young people were involved in the project through referrals from life skills training agencies and took part in a week-long residential programme. All participants were part of an on-going scheme with a firm support framework to ensure their continuing development as young adults. Conservation projects to engage vulnerable young people were identified through BTCV's existing networks. The feedback from the residentials was positive; all participants enjoyed the project and the majority felt that they had learned useful new skills as well increasing their confidence in both themselves and confidence in dealing with new skills and people. This work can really make a difference to young people's lives, helping to unlock potential that can remain hidden because they interact or learn in a different way.

The project involved a range of agencies working closely together which was vital to provide the support networks necessary for dealing with vulnerable groups. BTCV, Millennium Volunteers and Connexions were at the core of the project but it also involved Youth Services, Social Services and training organisations.

Planning is essential to ensure that barriers to participation are removed from the outset. One such example is the issue of obtaining parental consent. It is important to be clear about the realities of this type of work. Staff need to be flexible, but we need to remember they are not trained teachers or counsellors and it is important to understand where the boundaries lie. Effective partnerships with organisations with these skills are essential to bridge the gaps. This programme is intended to minimise the risk of working with such vulnerable groups, ensuring the quality and safety of the experience we provide for our volunteers is upheld.

Such examples of EfA projects undoubtedly bring many fantastic benefits to young people at risk of social exclusion, however, it is essential that substantial resources and commitment are in place for the project to be effectively delivered.

Anyone running a local project should always remember some key points:

- Never allow an adult volunteer to work alone with a young or vulnerable person;
- Encourage parents/guardians to work with their children.;
- Never take direct supervision of a group of children under the age of eight;
- If you are to supervise young or vulnerable people then there should be one trained leader/supervisor for every eight children between eight and 16 years of age. You should also have parental consent for them to be with you, for them to be carrying out conservation work and for emergency treatment at a hospital or doctors, should it be necessary; and
- You should always have a minimum of two leaders or supervisors on site.

Personal safety

Looking after yourself is certainly a health and safety issue! It's a responsibility for you and your employer, but it's largely up to you to look after yourself.

There are a few key areas that you should always bear in mind. As with all safety issues forward planning can remove many hazards.

Where are you going and why?

This may sound obvious, but if you're working in an unfamiliar area then you may be exposed to hazards and problems you've not thought about. You need back-up. If you are working as part of an organisation that is sending you out to work in a new area, then your manager should be ready to help. If you're working with one specific community group then you may not be so much at risk, but you should still take basic precautions. Remember that there are angry and hostile people in the world. If you are working with alienated communities or vulnerable groups you may come into contact with them. No-one should attend or be asked to attend what may be a hazardous meeting/event on their own. Bear in mind race and gender issues: some such events may indeed be more dangerous for some people than others, and respect people's concerns and fear over such matters.

If you are going to be on your own then discuss your concerns with your manager or committee and decide on the appropriate action. This may mean support from someone else, not attending an event or setting up a meeting at some other time.

Evening meetings

- Someone should always know where you're going and when you are expected back. This is certainly an issue for your manager.
- If you are going to an evening meeting, especially if it is in an unfamiliar location, arrange if possible to go there and back with a colleague.
- Take a mobile phone and numbers to ring in case of emergency.
- Sort out how you will get back: use a taxi if you have any concerns. Get the meeting organisers to sort one out if you are busy in the meeting so that it is ready and waiting when you finish.
- If you're cycling, make sure your bike is securely stored – bring it in to the meeting so that you can see it if need be.
- If you are going straight home after a potentially difficult visit arrange at least to phone a colleague to 'check in' at the office (if they are still there) or at home.

Other visits and meetings

- When meeting someone for the first time try to fix a first meeting in your office. If this is not possible ask for a telephone number and ring back to confirm the arrangement.
- Make sure you know as much as possible about the identity of the person you are going to see and that someone knows where you are going.
- Ensure that all work trips out of the office are recorded clearly in your schedule.
- If possible, during the winter arrange visits during the mornings only, so that they cannot extend into darkness.

- If you are on a site visit and it is clear that you are going to be back to the office later than anticipated, ring to let your colleagues know the situation and provide a new estimate of your anticipated return.
- If you are concerned about visiting a particular site, arrange for a colleague to accompany you – better to be safe than sorry.

DEALING WITH VIOLENT BEHAVIOUR

If you are working on a site where a violent or hostile situation develops take the greatest care if you become involved. Talk slowly and encourage those who are acting aggressively towards you or others to talk slowly as well. Let them vent their aggression, and be as understanding as you can, but don't make any promises that you cannot deliver. Resist any temptation to react aggressively. If knives or guns are produced or threatened then tell everyone else to leave the site, leave the site yourself and call the police.

If you feel you may be involved in this kind of situation then conflict resolution and assertiveness training will be very important.

General safety points

If you are about to be involved in work that may be hazardous:

- Think carefully how you are going to handle the work in order to reduce the likelihood of problems or conflict;
- When going to a meeting or visit that you think may be confrontational, discuss it with your manager or committee before going;
- Be aware of the effect which your style or dress may have on others. If you've got to build trust and confidence, start by thinking how people think about you; and
- Take an 'Outreach Bag' and a mobile phone (the contents of the outreach bag are outlined below).

The outreach bag

This idea originates with the Groundwork Trust in Medway Swale. It is simple and effective. Have a bag (perhaps a light day-pack) available in a designated place in the office with the emergency essentials you might need. This might include a torch, a notepad and pen, a waterproof, an alarm, a street map of the area as basics. A mobile phone won't live in the bag but should be considered an essential part of it. Add what you think necessary: this might include an envelope with enough money for a taxi across home and a phone card (for when the mobile gets stolen!), first aid materials if you are qualified, even a couple of bars of chocolate (often welcome after a shock. Simply pick up the bag as you leave the office (along with the phone).

Developing such a bag system for your office can be a useful exercise in safety awareness, but do make sure they are there (with all the essentials) when they are needed.

In 1998 the Estonia Fund for Nature (ELF) approached BTCV looking to work together to help ELF develop their own volunteer and community-based conservation programmes. Funding from the National Lottery enabled BTCV to work with partners in Eastern Europe helping them to develop their capacity to work with communities to care and manage their local environment. Through a programme of training and learning events, placements and joint projects, ELF very quickly gained the skills to develop and run their own projects and also transfer the skills gained from BTCV to others. One of these was a programme of support for the Kola Saami community.

The Kola Saami are an indigenous group living in the region of the Kola Peninsula, North West Russia. During the 1920s, the Soviet regime forced them to give up their historical lands and traditional reindeer-herding lifestyle in order to move them to more permanent settlements. The result was a loss of cultural identity and a reduction in numbers to about 1,800, of whom 900 now live in the village of Lovozero. The Saamis now suffer from social and economic problems, including unemployment, alcoholism and broken families. In recent years, however, they have started to set up community organisations, which are interested in starting some small-scale economic activity.

However, due to a lack of resources and experience this has proved very difficult. To overcome this, a capacity building project for Kola Saami community organisations was initiated locally by the Kildin Ancestral Community, with support from the Danish Foreign Ministry.

The project aims to strengthen the community organisations, and establish sustainable livelihoods for Kola Saami people in rural areas. It supports the organisational capacities of the Kildin Ancestral Community, establishing stronger networks, and initiating sustainable, small-scale economic activities (eg reindeer herding, sustainable tourism, handicraft production and community forestry). It promotes the restoration of ancestral land-use rights.

Training events and seminars have been held on topics such as community issues, public relations and project formulation capacities, sustainable tourism, reindeer-herding and community forestry. These seminars have brought together people from different Kola Saami communities, national NGOs and authorities. Study tours have also been conducted to Scandinavia and Estonia on reindeer-herding, sustainable tourism and organisational development.

The link between the Kola Saami community and Estonians began in the 1960s with various research projects on Kola Saami language and folklore. In 1988, the Estonian-Saami Society was founded to gather researchers, artists, musicians and other interested people. Since then, conferences, seminars, exhibitions, concerts have been arranged almost every year.

To initiate the Capacity Building project, a conference was held in September 2002 in the old Kola Saami village of Lovozero, an event partially funded by the Estonian Government. Accommodation was in traditional tipiis. The conference was preceded by a three-day clean-up action called 'Beautiful Tundra' where 50 high school students from Lovozero and volunteers from Estonia collected rubbish from around the conference site. It was also like an introduction to the concept of conservation holidays for the Kola Saami people, which was for them a novel concept. The conference was followed with a legal aid seminar about land-rights. At the seminar the Kola Saami community initiated the process of applying for a territory where they could practice the traditional use of natural resources.

The involvement of ELF (Estonian Fund for Nature) is related to its mission to support traditional land use as a way of preserving biodiversity for future generations. ELF's project manager Mikk Sarv had participated in many cultural projects with the Kola Saami and on one such visit to the Kola Peninsula offered to share with the Saami community the experiences ELF had gained during the its 11 years of existence, including skills in management, organisational development, PR work, project management, international co-operation gained from working with BTCV and other partners.

Part 3
Local action changes the world

Changing where I live

This guide is all about changing where you live. But when issues like climate change seems to need action at the highest as well as at personal levels, and governments seem to ignore international agreements, it can be hard to believe that actions any one of us take will really make a difference.

If you don't care about where you live, who will? The biggest challenge is perhaps to link the local action with the bigger global picture.

There is no doubt that local action does influence the bigger picture. There are plenty of examples where organised action by small groups has paved the way for much bigger change. It happened with the 'Montreal Protocol', the international agreement that has helped drastically reduce the amount of CFC gases being produced. On a wider scale, local and national action helped women obtain the vote, and even before that, the campaign to end slavery was started by a small group of people. So there is still hope for environmental change!

Governments pass laws, but making sure that those laws work is ultimately down to local people. Local councils will only really get active on basic issues such as fly-tipping if there is pressure on them from the community that is affected. Too many people think there's nothing they can do, but all the evidence shows that well-organised local action does work.

It's true that individuals can make an even bigger impact if they work together. Research published in 2002 for the Joseph Rowntree Foundation showed clearly that local projects do make a difference, not just in terms of the work they do but also through creating awareness and in encouraging more people to take action and get involved.

But, there's more to it than that. Many bigger local projects create jobs for local people and offer training that can help tackle the lack of skills and experience among unemployed people. Again, the impact of even a very good local project may be limited, but when you add them all together the impacts of such projects are certainly significant.

This was shown in 2002 when a national survey, 'The Quiet Revolution' published by the Shell Better Britain Campaign, showed just how much more work is being done now than 10 years ago. In 1992 there were less than 100 community projects refurbishing furniture and electrical goods for sale to people on low incomes. Now there are over 300 such programmes.

The same survey showed that there are 11,000 conservation groups of all shapes and sizes across the UK. In 1993 BTCV was working with less than 1,000 groups, by 2002 that figure was around 3,000. The number of community gardens and city farms has also grown steadily. The evidence shows that a great many people in Britain do care about the state of the environment and care enough to get out and do something about it.

Local action – making it work better

Despite all that action there's a lot more that can and needs to be done, and there are many more people and organisations who could do it. Some estimates suggest that there are as many as 750,000 community groups in the UK: as well as those 11,000 conservation groups, there are residents associations, youth groups, religious organisations, women's groups, and of course there are sports and leisure groups of all shapes and sizes, many of whom are out in local parks or other green spaces every week.

All those groups are made up of people who want to work with other people and who mostly share a desire to have a better quality of life. Yet relatively few of them are actively working on their local environment. That's a shame, but it is something that can be changed: perhaps one reason is that they don't feel that the environment has anything to do with them or believe that it's not their responsibility.

That is perhaps the biggest single challenge for local people who are active on these issues: to connect with all those people who care about where they live, but think that 'the environment' is something that you watch on television. The unfortunate fact is that all too often that perception has been helped by environment groups who have been seen as technical experts talking about over-complicated issues using incomprehensible jargon. It doesn't help that the traditional image of 'an environmentalist' is of a thoroughly well-meaning well-educated middle-class white person.

The environmental movement has certainly in the past been accused of caring far more about people's impact on the environment, than on the impact of a poor environment on people. This attitude is starting to change and needs to change more: that's not to say that concerns for the 'bigger picture' are not entirely justified, but they need to be linked to the concerns that are high on the list of people living in the very worst environments.

There are perhaps three important issues that anyone interested in developing environmental work, that is genuinely inclusive, needs to think about. The first of these is in terms of how those working on environmental issues can work effectively with other professions and disciplines operating in the same area. The second concerns the environmental inequalities that exist in our society and ways to tackle these through an 'environmental justice' approach. The last focuses on how our work locally links to and supports work on global concerns.

Caring in the community?

After many years of neglect, the Government has realised that our neighbourhoods, our parks and our play spaces are all too often uncared for and run down. More money is now available but it needs more than money and one or two more council staff: it needs the people who use those spaces to get active – not just to complain about the problems, but to help plan and manage the solutions.

This guide shows how you and anyone else can get projects moving to change where you live. And if you are keen to do that we've also shown that involving the wider local community need not be too difficult.

Of course many local projects have other priorities: tackling deprivation and ill-health, providing better facilities for young or older people, working with ethnic minority communities and so on, but all of them are affected to some extent by the quality of the local environment. If it's unpleasant and unsafe people are less likely to want to go out and socialise.

Sharing concerns and broadening vision

If environmental action is going to prosper and build better links with people and community groups with other concerns, then it's important to understand their concerns and link to them. That means a little less talking about how bad the environmental problems are and more listening to the social problems in order to find actions and projects that can help resolve both.

Building such interdisciplinary links is not always easy. Anyone seeking to involve community groups in environmental action may need to develop an understanding of anti-poverty and child education targets as well as health priorities. Each discipline is looking to see stronger communities but each is also looking to meet its own targets

WORKING ACROSS THE ISSUES

A good example of projects that can help work across both issues is BTCV Green Gym. These projects combine practical conservation work with activities to help participants keep fit and stay healthy. The first was set up in 1997 as a joint venture between Sonning Common Health Centre, Oxfordshire, and BTCV to encourage the local community to improve both their health and environment.

There are now over 60 BTCV Green Gym projects across the UK. The participants benefit their health by taking part in conservation activities which, in turn, benefits the health of the environment. So, for example, walkers benefit by upgrading footpaths to encourage easier and safer walking.

Although the scheme can be compared to GP Referral schemes run in leisure centres, people wear ordinary clothes, use inexpensive equipment and can see a tangible result in their good work. Drop-out rates are low with an adherence rate of 72%.

The BTCV Green Gym programme is continuously evaluated by Oxford Brookes University and shows that this kind of work could produce significant improvements in cardiovascular fitness, as well as mental health benefits, so long as participants work on a regular basis.

It can be hard for community projects to make these links: one way to do so may be to build better links with your local council or health agency. Most councils have an environmental or sustainability development officer who will probably have a good knowledge and understanding of what is going on in your locality. They may be able to provide advice on which groups may share your interests or concerns. Many councils also have some form of local sustainability network or forum, or Local Strategic Partnership, which is a very good way of meeting other organisations; it can also be a way for you to feed your concerns into local decision-making.

One way of developing an integrated approach to do this is to write down evaluation questions (see Part 2.8) that will help show how any project is helping deliver benefits not just for the environment but also for other community priorities. To do this successfully, you will probably need assistance from people in those other disciplines so that you can be sure you are measuring the issues that they think are important.

Sharing everyone's concerns

There's a second issue to be tackled by any project looking to really link in to the bigger picture. Parts 2.3 and 2.4 look at how you can build better links with different groups within a locality, but it's also important to consider the underlying issues. It's often the case that the most deprived people live in the worst environments. This can make life even more problematic – it can affect people's health, cause mental stress and can also put off businesses that might invest in an area and create jobs.

You can find out more about areas of deprivation and indicators of deprivation by talking to the sustainability officer at the local council, or by checking out the Regional Development Agency website where there will be information covering the whole of your region.

There's plenty of evidence that this link between poverty and poor environments is widespread, and that it is not a coincidence. Polluting installations, whether they are waste management sites or chemical factories, have to be built somewhere, and when something of this nature is planned it's usually the rich and the well-educated who can kick up the most fuss. The result, unsurprisingly, is that the poor get the worst of it. Friends of the Earth research linked the Government Index of Multiple Deprivation with industrial emissions data from the Environment Agency. In 1999 11,400 tonnes of carcinogenic chemicals were released in to the atmosphere, and 82% came from factories located in the most deprived 20% of local authority wards.

And it's not just about being poor. Similar work by the University of Staffordshire found a significant bias whereby polluting sites are located in wards with a substantial ethnic minority population (70% of all people from ethnic minorities live in the 88 most deprived local council areas).

Work is now being done to tackle these environmental inequalities, and the idea of 'environmental justice' is at the heart of this work.

Environmental justice is a phrase developed in the USA over 20 years ago, where research showed that environmental pollution had a disproportionate effect on black and ethnic minority communities. Furthermore, racial disparities (black communities suffering an unfair impact) were more common that ones relating to poverty. This has led to a range of action to reduce discrimination and a serious shake-ups in the environmental movement which was accused of having failed to respond to the needs of black communities.

In 2003, environmental justice moved onto the UK agenda. The Government is (at the time of writing) consulting on the new sustainable development strategy for the UK, and environmental justice is one of the key themes for that work. Regeneration programmes are now looking to research and tackle environmental inequalities alongside health inequalities. It's an issue that any local project should look at in their neighbourhood.

However, it's not just an issue about polluting factories: environmental inequalities relate to many other more mundane issues, such as air pollution, noise, access to green spaces, and access to public transport. English Nature wants everyone to have adequate access to 'Natural Green Space', which they define as 'land, water or geological features which have been naturally colonised by plants and animals, and which are accessible on foot to large numbers of people'.

They recommend that people living in towns and cities should have such a green space with 300 metres from their home. By no means everyone has such access, and improving the quality of local green space (or creating a new one) could be the task for a local project which could then help meet this target and thus help minimise environmental inequalities.

At its heart, environmental justice is a very different way of looking at the environment – one that is based on our right to enjoy safe and healthy surroundings, rather than on tackling specific issues about pollution, transport or biodiversity. This integrated approach also links closely to the principles of sustainable development and to the underlying idea of EfA.

The global agenda
Even if our local project is one of thousands and collectively we are having a significant impact, it can be hard to see how what we are doing affects global issues such as climate change, environmental justice, world trade, global development and so on.

There is no simple and comprehensive answer to this question, but there are a lot of small answers. Much of what we do in our daily lives affects other countries, most notably through what we buy and consume. The UN's Agenda 21 report for the 1992 Earth Summit spelled it out directly: 'the major cause of the continued deterioration of the global environment is the unsustainable pattern of production and consumption, particularly in industrialized countries.' We are the problem, and it's up to us to play what part we can in creating more sustainable ways to live and consume.

How we use energy is one place to start. We use huge amounts of oil, causing pollution in its production, transport and final use, but we also waste around a third of the energy we use. To make matters worse, millions of poorer households in the UK are in a state of 'fuel poverty', which means that they spend more than 10% of their income on energy. We can all take steps to cut down on our own energy waste (and thus save some money) and community groups can do a lot more. In Brighton, a network of community groups have looked at how their community centres can become energy-efficient buildings, while all over the UK there are Energy Advice Centres and other local projects underway.

However, there's a lot more to be done, especially in terms of helping 'hard-to-reach' households – people who are poor, newly arrived refugees, people who speak little or no English and so on. A project may seek to involve these groups in a conservation task, but could also use the contacts they have made through this work to provide advice on energy saving (and waste recycling).

But it's not the poor who are the problem. The people who are using the most energy are the wealthy in larger houses with one or more cars, for whom the electricity bill is just another bill to be paid. Yet if we are to tackle climate change it's consumption patterns like this that need to be tackled and any local organisation can certainly play a part, by making people aware of the issues and providing advice and support for those starting to change how they live.

Another good example of how we can change where we live is by examining the food we eat. Fresh food is good for us, and locally-produced fresh food also cuts down on transport costs and pollution. Therefore, why not grow more locally? There are now hundreds of local food-growing projects, along with over 8,000 allotment sites and around 350 'farmers' markets' which sell locally-grown produce. Any project looking to improve a piece of land might want to look at how that land could be used to produce food: there are many underused sites around the UK, much of it close to or in housing estates. Many of the people who said 'it can't be done' are now eating fresh food they've grown themselves.

We all do live on the same planet, although its resources are shared very unequally. While we worry about our 'own backyard', we should also remember that there's also a very big front yard – and that all our front doors are open on to it. We may not choose to worry about global problems, but we can certainly act if we choose. Local action may seem to have only limited effects, but if we don't take action, then we shouldn't expect anyone else to. And, if we do take action, then we take a first step towards making the changes we want to see happen.

Hopefully this guide has provided you with advice and ideas, not just on taking the first step, but also on going forward to helping create a community in which you are happy to live, and a place that respects and enhances both the local and global environments.

Glossary

Age Concern – The largest UK organisation working with and for older people.

Big Lottery Fund – A new organisation created by the merging of The Community Fund and the New Opportunities Fund that deals with National Lottery funding for good causes.

Black Environment Network (BEN) – Established to promote Equality of Opportunity with respect to ethnic communities in the preservation, protection, and development of the environment.

BCTV Green Gym® – Offers people the opportunity to carry out worthwhile practical conservation work, whilst enjoying the health benefits of tailored exercise programmes and 'working out' in the open air. BTCV Green Gyms help to tackle long-term health problems through a programme of environmental activities. Individuals join in weekly sessions of gardening, walling and many other activities that help them to improve their health and sense of well-being.

Community Development Foundation – Set out to develop and promote informal activity in local communities that are not usually reached by the agencies that are concerned with more formal volunteering.

Council for Voluntary Service (CVS) – Network of over 300 Councils for Voluntary Service (CVS) throughout England. They help to promote voluntary and community action by supporting the member CVS and by acting as a national voice for the local voluntary and community sector.

The Countryside Agency – An agency working to make the quality of life better for people in the countryside; and the quality of the countryside better for everyone.

Criminal Records Bureau (CRB) – The CRB is the branch of the Home Office set up for the purpose of helping organisations make safe recruitment choices.

Energy Advice Centres – Service centres to promote energy conservation, the use of renewable energy and provide independent advice and information.

Environmental Agency – The Environmental Agency works for the betterment of surroundings for different regions and peoples of the UK, promoting a better environment for current and future generations.

Equal Opportunities Employer – A company that follows guidelines to wipe out discrimination of race, sex, age, etc.

Friends of the Earth – An organisation that encourages solutions to environmental problems improving the quality of life for more people.

Government Index of Multiple Deprivation – Measures deprivation for every Super Output Area and local authority area in England. It combines indicators across seven domains into a single deprivation score and rank. Domains included are: income deprivation, employment deprivation, health deprivation and disability, education, skills and training deprivation, barriers to housing services, living environment deprivation, and crime. Sometimes just known as 'indices of deprivation'.

Groundwork – A leading environmental regeneration charity making sustainable development a reality in communities in the UK which are in need of investment and support.

Joseph Rowntree Foundation – An organisation that conducts research and development programmes that seek to better understand the causes of social difficulties and explore ways of better overcoming them.

The Muslim Council – Aims to promote cooperation, consensus, and unity on Muslim affairs in the UK.

Race Relations Act – An Act of Parliament constructed to fight discrimination. Original Act 1976. Amended 2000.

Race Equality Council (REC) – Local councils that work among communities to promote racial equality and tackle racial discrimination.

RADAR – A society that promotes change by encouraging disabled people to achieve their rights and expectations. It is also working to change the way the disabled are viewed by the public.

Refugee Council – The largest organisation in the UK working with asylum seekers and refugees.

Regional Development Agency – Local agencies responsible for the sustainable economic development and regeneration of regions of the UK. Priorities include: business development, regeneration, skills and employment, infrastructure and image.

Sensory Trust – The Sensory Trust is an organisation that promotes and implements inclusive environmental design and management.

Shell Better Britain Campaign – Campaign supported by Working for Environmental Community Action Now (WECAN!). The campaign provides a package of information and grants designed to encourage more people to embrace the principles of sustainability as they carry out local activities to improve their environment. Now obsolete.

Thrive – The national horticultural charity that exists to enable disadvantaged, disabled and older people to participate fully in the social and economic life of the community.

United Nations 'Earth Summit' (1992) – United Nations Conference held in Brazil in 1992 to discuss environment and sustainable development. Sometimes known simply as 'Rio'.

WWF – A global organisation that acts locally through a network of family offices striving towards halting the accelerating destruction of our natural world.

Contacts

Active Communities Unit
Home Office, Room 236, Horseferry House,
Dean Ryle Street, London SW1P 2AW
Tel: 0207 7035 5331
Web: www.homeoffice.gov.uk

Age Concern
Astral House, 1268 London Road, London SW16 4ER
Tel: 020 8765 7200
Web: www.ageconcern.org.uk

Big Lottery Fund
1 Plough Place, London EC4A 1DE
Tel: 020 7211 1800
Web: www.biglotteryfund.org.uk

Black Environment Network (BEN)
9 Llainwen Uchaf, Llanberis, Wales LL55 4LL
Tel: 01286 870 715
E: BEN@ben-network.demon.co.uk
Web: www.ben-network.org

CABE
The Tower Building, 11 York Road, London SE1 7NX
Tel: 0207 960 2400
Web: www.cabespace.org.uk

Centre For Sustainable Energy
The CREATE Centre, Smeaton Road,
Bristol BSI 6XN
Tel: 0117 929 9950
E: info@cse.org.uk; Web: www.cse.org.uk

Charity Commission
Harmsworth House, 13-15 Bouverie Street
London EC4Y 8DP

Tel: 0870 333 0123
Web: www.charitycommission.gov.uk

Commission for Racial Equality (CRE)
St Dunstan's House, 201-211 Borough High Street
London SE1 1GZ
Tel: 0207 939 0000
E: info@cre.gov.uk; Web: www.cre.gov.uk

Community Development Foundation
60 Highbury Grove, London N5 2AG
Tel: 0207 226 5375
E: admin@cdf.org.uk; Web: www.cdf.org.uk

The Countryside Agency
Tel: 01242 521 381
E: info@countryside.gov.uk
Web: www.countryside.gov.uk

Countryside Council for Wales
Maes-y-Ffynnon, Penrhosgarnedd, Bangor
Gwynedd LL57 2DW
Tel: 0845 130 6229
Web: www.ccw.gov.uk

Criminal Records Bureau
Customer Services, CRB, PO Box 110,
Liverpool L69 3EF
Tel: 0870 909 0811
Web: www.crb.gov.uk

Defra
Nobel House, 17 Smith Square,
London SW1P 3JR
Tel: 0207 238 6000
Web: www.defra.gov.uk

DoE Northern Ireland
DOE Headquarters, Clarence Court,
10–18 Adelaide Street, Belfast BT2 8GB
Tel: 028 9054 0540
Web: www.doeni.gov.uk

Directory of Social Change
24 Stephenson Way, London NW1 2DP
Tel: 0207 209 5151
Web: www.dsc.org.uk

English Nature
Northminster House, Peterborough PE1 1UA
Tel: 01733 455000
Web: www.english-nature.org.uk

The Environment Council
212 High Holborn, London WC1V 7BF
Tel: 0207 836 2626
Web: www.the-environment-council.org.uk

Environmental Agency
Tel: 0870 850 6506
Web: www.environment-agency.gov.uk

Friends of the Earth
26-28 Underwood Street, London N1 7JQ
Tel: 0808 800 1111
E: info@foe.co.uk; Web: www.foe.co.uk

Groundwork UK
85-87 Cornwall Street, Birmingham B3 3BY
Tel: 0121 236 8565
E: info@groundwork.org.uk
Web: www.groundwork.org.uk

Health and Safety Executive
HSE, Caerphilly Business Park, Caerphilly CF83 3GG
Tel: 0870 154 5500
Web: www.hse.gov.uk

Home Office
Home Office, Direct Communications Unit,
7th Floor, 50 Queen Anne's Gate
London SW1H 9AT
Tel: 0870 000 1585
Hard of hearing textphone: 0207 273 3476
E: public.enquiries@homeoffice.gsi.gov.uk
Web: www.homeoffice.gov.uk

Inland Revenue
Tel: 0845 714 3143
Web: www.inlandrevenue.gov.uk

The Institute of Linguists
Educational Trust, Saxon House, 48 Southwark Street
London SE1 1UN
Tel: 0207 940 3100
Web: www.iol.org.uk

Institute for Volunteering Research
Regent's Wharf, 8 All Saints Street, London N1 9RL
Tel: 0207 520 8900
Web: www.ivr.org.uk

The Interfaith Network
5-7 Tavistock Place, London, WC1H 9SN
Tel: 0207 388 0008 (NI: 028 9038 4328)
Web: www.interfaith.org.uk

Joseph Rowntree Foundation
The Homestead, 40 Water End, York,
North Yorkshire YO30 6WP
Tel: 01904 629 241
Web: www.jrf.org.uk

The Muslim Council
Suite 5, Boardman House, 64 Broadway,
Stratford, London E15 1NT
Tel: 0208 432 0585/6
E: admin@mcb.org.uk; Web: www.mcb.org.uk

MIND
15-19 Broadway, London E15 4BQ
Tel: 0208 519 2122
Web: www.mind.org.uk

National Association of Councils for Voluntary Service
177 Arundel Street, Sheffield S1 2NU
Tel: 0114 278 6636
Textphone: 0114 278 7025
E: nacvs@nacvs.org.uk; Web: www.nacvs.org.uk

National Federation of City Farms
The Greenhouse, Hereford Street, Bedminster
Bristol BS3 4NA
Tel: 0117 923 1800

The NI Volunteer Development Agency
Annsgate House, 70-74 Ann St Belfast BT1 4EH
Tel 028 9023 6100
Web: www.volunteering-ni.org

RADAR
Head Office, 12 City Forum , 250 City Road,
London EC1V 8AF
Tel: 0207 250 3222
E: radar@radar.org.uk; Web: www.radar.org.uk

Refugee Council
3 Bondway, London, SW8 1SJ
Tel: 0207 820 3000
Web: www.refugeecouncil.org.uk

Refugee Integration Unit
Home Office, 4th Floor, Apollo House,
36 Wellesley Road, Croydon CR9 3RR
Tel: 0208 760 8570

Regional Development Agencies
Web: www.englandsrdas.com

Royal National Institute of the Blind
105 Judd Street, London WC1H 9NE
Tel: 0207 388 1266
Web: www.rnib.org.uk

Scottish Natural Heritage
12 Hope Terrace, Edinburgh EH9 2AS
Tel: 0131 447 4784
Web: www.snh.org.uk

Scottish Refugee Council
5 Cadogan Square, 170 Blythswood Court
Glasgow G2 7PH
Tel: 0141 248 9799
Web: www.scottishrefugeecouncil.org.uk

Sensory Trust
Watering Lane Nursery, Pentewan, St Austell,
Cornwall PL26 6BE
E: enquiries@sensorytrust.org.uk
Web: www.sensorytrust.org.uk

Thrive
The Geoffrey Udall Centre, Beech Hill,
Reading RG7 2AT
Tel: 0118 988 5688
E: info@thrive.org.uk

WWF
Panda House, Weyside Park,
Godalming, Surrey GU7 1XR
Tel: 01483 426 444
E: questions@wwfint.org; Web: www.wwf.org

Have you tried BTCV's online shop yet?

At BTCV, we are committed to improving our service to supporters and customers. We hope that our online one-stop shop for BTCV products and services will equip you for your work with community groups.

You can now buy all the **tools and equipment** you might need for community conservation work at the same time.

We also supply **trees, shrubs and wildflowers**.

We offer a specially negotiated public liability **insurance** package for community groups and other cover required for practical environmental action.

As well as this guide, BTCV offers **training courses**, and our **books** provide authoritative information on a range of practical conservation techniques and habitats.

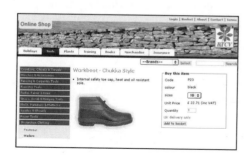

www.btcv.org/shop

"I can't recommend BTCV's Insurance package highly enough!"

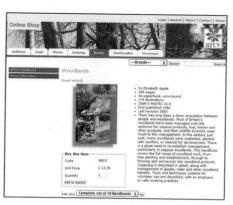

INSPIRING PEOPLE, IMPROVING PLACES

Reg. charity 261009   Registered office: BTCV, Conservation Centre, Balby Rd, Doncaster DN4 0RH

Publications and websites

RECOMMENDED PUBLICATIONS

The A-Z of Volunteering and Asylum
A Handbook for Managers. Ruth Wilson.

Community Research: Getting Started
ARVAC. 2002.

Governance in Focus
A Race and Gender Perspective. Tesse Akpeki

Recruiting Volunteers: attracting the people you need
Directory of Social Change.
Dyer, Fraser and Jost. 2002.

Faith and Volunteering Action: communities, resources and values
Mike Locke and Priya Lukka with Andri
Soteri-Procter. NCV. 2003.

As Good as Your Word
A Guide to community interpreting and translation in public services. Marsha Sanders. Maternity Alliance. 2000.

The Diversity Training Handbook
John Jones and Phil Clements. Kogan Page. 2002.

Volunteering for All?
Exploring the Link between Volunteering and Social Exclusion – Institute for Volunteering Research.

(you can view the whole text at **www.ivr.org.uk**)

Saving Open Space
How to run a Successful Community Campaign to Save Open Space. Green Space. 2004.

Young refugees: setting up youth groups for young refugees in the UK
Save the Children, 2003.
Save the Children, 17 Grove Lane, London SE5 8RD
Tel: 0208 741 4054
Web: www.savethechildren.org.uk

The Good Practice Guide
The National Centre for Volunteering, Regent's Wharf
8 All Saints Street, London N1 9RL
Web: www.volunteering.org.uk

GreenSpace has several useful publications available from www.green-space.org.uk

Free introductory leaflets on fundraising from trusts and foundations are available from **The Association of Charitable Foundations**, which is the umbrella organisation for UK grant-making trusts and foundations: www.acf.org.uk

Faith Communities Toolkit
Faith in London for Jobcentre Plus
1 King Edwards Road, London, E8 7SF
Tel: 0208 510 0440 E: info@faithinlondon.org

RECOMMENDED WEBSITES

The Office for National Statistics produces a wide range of key economic and social statistics – particularly useful when evidence of demographic profiles are needed. www.statistics.gov.uk

The Office of the Deputy Prime Minister (ODPM) has information on the Index of Deprivation, which contains useful facts and figures on identifying areas in need of community work and regeneration.
www.odpm.gov.uk
The ODPM also has a site on social exclusion at www.socialexclusionunit.gov.uk

The New Policy Institute runs a site that monitors what is happening to poverty and social exclusion in the UK and complements their annual monitoring reports. The material is organised around 50 statistical indicators covering all aspects of the subject, from income and work to health and education.
www.poverty.org.uk/intro

Directory of Social Change (DSC) was established in 1975 to help voluntary and community organisations become more effective, and to promote positive social change. It gives access to government grants for the voluntary and community sector.
www.governmentfunding.org.uk

Department for Education and Skills
www.dfes.gov.uk

Institute of Fundraising
http://www.institute-of-fundraising.org.uk

NINIS provides free access to statistical and locational information relating to small areas across Northern Ireland. The Northern Ireland Statistics and Research Agency (NISRA) is Northern Ireland's official statistics organisation.
www.ninis.nisra.gov.uk

Scottish Neighbourhood Statistics
This service is being used to inform the Scottish Executive's approach to improving the quality of life for people living in Scotland and especially in the most disadvantaged areas.
www.sns.gov.uk

Neighbourhood Statistics Service
www.neighbourhood.statistics.gov.uk

Community Foundations are grant-making trusts that are owned and managed by communities.
www.communityfoundations.org.uk

A free searchable online directory of grants helps you locate grants relevant to your needs.
www.grantsnet.co.uk

An annual subscription to www.trustfunding.org.uk will allow access to relevant funding sources.

BTCV publications

BTCV's series of books was started in the 1970s, with most of the original titles remaining in print throughout and new titles being added over the years. There is a rolling programme of revision and BTCV welcomes feedback at any time on any aspect of our publications, whether the comments are general or detailed, practical or academic, complimentary or critical. Please contact:

Handbooks Editor, BTCV, Howbery Park, Wallingford, Oxfordshire OX10 8BA.

Tel: 01491 821605

Fax 01491 839646

E: information@btcv.org.uk

...or comment online at www.btcv.org/handbooks

Titles include:
Dry Stone Walling, Fencing, Footpaths, Hedging, Sand Dunes, Tool Care, Tree Planting and Aftercare, The Urban Handbook, Waterways and Wetlands, Woodlands.

To order, contact:
BTCV,
Conservation Centre,
Balby Road,
Doncaster DN4 0RH
Tel: 01302 572200
Web: www.btcv.org

Will you help us to achieve our goals?

BTCV needs your help. Will you support us? Every penny you give will help us to provide professional advice and support needed to give more people the opportunity to improve their place and, through this, the global environment.

Your contribution is vital for us to continue to inspire, engage and equip people, to take practical action to create a more sustainable future.

- Enrich the lives of **1 million people**, through involvement with BTCV, volunteering opportunities, employment, improved health, and life skill development.

- Improve the biodiversity and local environment of **20,000 places**.

- Support active citizenship in **5,000 community-based groups**.

INSPIRING PEOPLE, IMPROVING PLACES

Reg. charity 261009   Registered office: BTCV, Conservation Centre, Balby Rd, Doncaster DN4 0RH

I WANT TO HELP
Please tick the appropriate box(es) below and send to: BTCV, Freepost SEA13250, Ashford, Kent TN23 1YU

☐ YES, I would like to support BTCV's work with a donation of ☐ £20 ☐ £80 ☐ £190 ☐ £250 Other:

☐ I enclose a cheque made out to BTCV   ☐ Please debit my Vis/Mastercard/CAF Charity Card (delete as appropriate)

Card Number
☐☐☐☐ ☐☐☐☐ ☐☐☐☐ ☐☐☐☐ ☐☐☐☐   Expiry Date ☐☐ ☐☐

Signature _____ Date _____

Name & Address _____

GIFT AID DECLARATION Using Gift Aid means that for every pound you give we get an extra 28p back from the Inland Revenue. You must pay an amount of income tax or capital gains tax at least equal to the tax BTCV reclaims on your donations in the tax year (currently 28p for each £1 you give)

☐ YES, I would like BTCV to treat all donations I have made since 6 April 2000, and all I make from now on until I notify you otherwise, as Gift Aid donation (please be sure to sign, right)   Signature _____ Date _____

We are also actively seeking partnerships with companies to help deliver corporate social responsibility objectives that really make a difference to people's lives. Call us on 01302 572244 to find out more.

Notes

Notes